CRICKET'S CHOICE

Edited by Clifton Fadiman and Marianne Carus

Open Court
La Salle, Illinois

Printed in the United States of America

ISBN: 0-87548-318-6

Library of Congress Catalog Card Number: 74-18355

Grateful acknowledgement is given to the following publishers and copyright owners for permission granted to reprint selections from their publications. All possible care has been taken to trace ownership and secure permission for each selection included.

George Adamson and Faber & Faber, Ltd. for illustrations for "Meet My Folks" from *Meet My Folks* by Ted Hughes, copyright © 1961, 1973 by Ted Hughes.
The Bobbs-Merrill Co., Inc. for introduction and three poems for "Meet My Folks" from *Meet My Folks* by Ted Hughes, copyright © 1961, 1973 by Ted Hughes.
Brandt & Brandt for "The True Enchanter" from *The Foundling and Other Tales of Prydain* by Lloyd Alexander, published by Holt, Rinehart & Winston, Inc., copyright © 1973 by Lloyd Alexander.
Curtis Brown, Ltd. for "Tyrannosaurus Rex" from *The Old Dog Barks Backwards* by Ogden Nash, published by Little Brown & Co., copyright © 1969 by Ogden Nash; English translation by Doris Orgel of "Cats," English translation copyright © 1974 by Doris Orgel; illustration by Cyndy Szekeres for "Valentine," copyright © 1974 by Open Court Publishing Co.; illustrations by Cyndy Szekeres for "The Neat Raccoon and the Untidy Owl," copyright © 1974 by Open Court Publishing Co.; illustration by Cyndy Szekeres for "The Last Word of a Bluebird," copyright © 1973 by Open Court Publishing Co.; and illustrations by Jan Adkins for "The Day Grandfather Tickled a Tiger," copyright © 1974 by Jan Adkins.
Eve Bunting for "A Fish for Finn" by Eve Bunting, copyright © 1974 by Eve Bunting.
Natalie Savage Carlson for "The Neat Raccoon and the Untidy Owl" by Natalie Savage Carlson, copyright © 1974 by Natalie Savage Carlson.

contents

Old Cricket
INVITES YOU
TO A BIRTHDAY PARTY

Whether you're young, old, or somewhere in-between, you're invited to a birthday party. As these words are written, *Cricket: The Magazine for Children* is one year old, and *Cricket's Choice* is our way of celebrating its happy first anniversary. During the year we published nine issues. It is from these that the contents of *Cricket's Choice* are drawn.

What is *Cricket*?

It's a magazine for children, as well as for those grown-ups who are still children at heart. (There are even some teen-agers who read *Cricket* on the sly.)

For children—but perhaps not for all children. It's for those who really delight in using their minds and imaginations.

Cricket publishes the best stories, articles, and art it can get from the best children's writers and artists in the world. Many of these are represented in this anniversary book. Here are Carl Sandburg, Lloyd Alexander, Elizabeth Coatsworth, Gwendolyn Brooks, Eleanor Estes, Isaac Bashevis Singer, Robert Frost, and many others from our own country; Farley Mowat from Canada; Gianni Rodari from Italy; Kornei Chukovsky from Soviet Russia; T.S. Eliot, Helen Cresswell, Walter de la Mare, Philippa Pearce, Ted Hughes, James Reeves, and others from England; Hans Baumann and Christian Morgenstern from Germany; Alf Prøysen from Sweden; and two Jameses (Stephen and Joyce) from Ireland. A great many of the contributors are prize-winning authors. (You'll find a list at the end of the book.) There's also William Shakespeare, not a prize-winner, but otherwise favorably known.

Cricket's Choice will give old readers the pleasure of seeing some of their favorites collected between the covers of one book. But, more especially, it will show new readers just what *Cricket* is up to, and what sort of stories, poems, and art these readers can expect in future issues.

In *Cricket's Choice* there are funny poems about cats and bones and bugs and snails and the letter W. There are serious poems about a cricket and a November sunset and the Three Wise Men. There's a story about a fierce, fiery fox and a song about one, too. There are scary stories (try *The Yellow Ribbon* on Halloween), and nonsense stories (my favorites are *Mrs. Pepperpot* and *Little Green Riding Hood*). There are puzzles and tongue twisters and a recipe for sugar cookies (delicious!). There's news about shooting stars and Mary Poppins and the Abominable Snowman and the table manners of children 500 years ago. There are directions for seeing floating frankfurters. There are legends and fairy tales and puppet plays and animal storeis. And there are pictures. "What is the use of a book without pictures?" asked Alice in Wonderland.

We hope this book will introduce new readers to *Cricket*, and that *Cricket* will become an old friend. If you like *Cricket's Choice* I'd love to hear from you. You can just address me as *Old Cricket*, Box 100, La Salle, Illinois 61301. I'll get your letters—the mailman and I are friends.

Clifton Fadiman

CRICKET'S CHOICE

Toad's Garden
by Arnold Lobel HE DREW THE PICTURES TOO!

Frog was in his garden.
Toad came walking by.
"What a fine garden
you have, Frog," he said.

"Yes," said Frog. "It is very nice,
but it was hard work."
"I wish I had a garden," said Toad.
"Here are some flower seeds.
Plant them in the ground," said Frog,
"and soon you will have a garden."
"How soon?" asked Toad.
"Quite soon," said Frog.
Toad ran home.
He planted the flower seeds.
"Now seeds," said Toad,
"start growing."
Toad walked up and down
a few times.
The seeds did not start to grow.

Toad put his head
close to the ground
and said loudly,
"Now seeds, start growing!"
Toad looked at the ground again.
The seeds did not start to grow.
Toad put his head
very close to the ground and shouted,
"NOW SEEDS, START GROWING!"
Frog came running up the path.
"What is all this noise?" he asked.
"My seeds will not grow," said Toad.
"You are shouting too much,"
said Frog. "These poor seeds
are afraid to grow."
"My seeds are afraid to grow?"
asked Toad.

"Of course," said Frog.
"Leave them alone for a few days.
Let the sun shine on them,
let the rain fall on them.
Soon your seeds will start to grow."

That night
Toad looked out of his window.
"Drat!" said Toad.

"My seeds have not
started to grow.

They must be afraid of the dark."
Toad went out to his garden
with some candles.
"I will read the seeds a story,"
said Toad.
"Then they will not be afraid."
Toad read a long story
to his seeds.

All the next day
Toad sang songs
to his seeds.

And all the next day
Toad read poems
to his seeds.

And all the next day
Toad played music
for his seeds.

Toad looked at the ground.
The seeds still did not
start to grow.
"What shall I do?" cried Toad.
"These must be
the most frightened seeds
in the whole world!"
Then Toad felt very tired,
and he fell asleep.

"Toad, Toad, wake up," said Frog.
"Look at your garden!"
Toad looked at his garden.
Little green plants were coming up
out of the ground.

"At last," shouted Toad, "my seeds have stopped being afraid to grow!" "And now you will have a nice garden too," said Frog. "Yes," said Toad, "but you were right, Frog. It was very hard work."

The End

Ship Ahoy!

PAUL GALDONE DREW THIS. (HE'S A SWEETHEART!)

by Hans Baumann

Characters

CASPAR	BROOM
TOPKNOT	LAZY DEVIL

In Caspar's house. Caspar and his friend Topknot in bed, head to toe, under a bedspread. A clock strikes ten.

CASPAR (*Sitting up*): Oooh-er-ah! Ten o'clock already! Topknot, I must shake a leg.

TOPKNOT: Why, Caspar? Bed's best.

CASPAR: And who's going to clean? I have to clean before Grandma comes back.

TOPKNOT: Am I your best friend? Or am I not?

12

WALTER
LORRAINE
DREW THESE CRAZY
PUPPET PICTURES!

CASPAR: You are, Topknot. You are my best friend.

TOPKNOT: Then you aren't going to leave your best friend.

CASPAR: I don't want to—but Grandma said—

TOPKNOT (*Interrupting*): Fiddlesticks!

CASPAR: You shouldn't talk like that about Grandma.

TOPKNOT: I'll talk how I like! And I won't let you get up.

CASPAR: You see how it is, children? I'm dying to get up—but my friend Topknot won't let me.

BROOM (*Dancing about in the corner*): Caspar, come and get me!

CASPAR: Who's that? Who said that?

BROOM: Me! Broom! It's high time you picked me up. Or you won't be ready when Grandma comes back. And then you won't get your doughnut!

CASPAR: I'm coming. (*He tries to get up.*)

TOPKNOT (*Holding him back*):   I won't let you go! I won't! I won't!

CASPAR: You see, Broom! I want to come and get you—but my friend Topknot won't let me. You'd better come to me instead.

BROOM: I can't move unless you come and get me.

TOPKNOT: Ha ha ha! Ha ha ha!

CASPAR: What's so funny?

TOPKNOT: I'm laughing at that broom. It's getting no-where—and neither are you!

CASPAR: You're a fine friend today! You're not at all like your usual self.

BROOM: I know why—there's something behind it.

14

CASPAR: What's behind what?

BROOM: Behind your friend's bad mood. Do you know what you have to do? You have to beat him up a little.

CASPAR: Beat him up a little?

BROOM: Right.

CASPAR: Beat up my friend Topknot?

BROOM: Biff him and bash him! Shake him and smash him!

CASPAR: What has he done to deserve that?

BROOM (*Dancing about*):

Biff him and smash him,
Bash him about!
Something's got into him.
You beat it out!

CASPAR: Why do I have to beat it out, Topknot? Why can't you just tell me what's got into you?

TOPKNOT: What's got into me? I'll tell you what's . . . (*He shivers and shakes.*) Ow! Ow! Ow!

CASPAR: What are you yelling like that for?

TOPKNOT: Because. . .Ow!

CASPAR: For goodness' sake, Topknot! Tell me!

TOPKNOT: I can't.

CASPAR: Then you aren't my best friend at all.

TOPKNOT: Fiddledy-fiddlesticks!

CASPAR: Fiddlesticks yourself!

TOPKNOT: Fiddlesticks to you!

CASPAR: And you! (*They begin hitting each other. Caspar rolls his friend Topknot out of bed and shakes him. A little devil pops out.*) Look at that! It's a sort of little devil, isn't it?

TOPKNOT: I can't tell you.

BROOM: But *I* can! It's the lazybones devil, Bones-ebub.

CASPAR: Who's Bones-ebub?

BROOM: One of the five thousand lazy devils who stop people from getting up in the morning.

CASPAR: Is that right, Topknot?

TOPKNOT: Yes, that's right.

CASPAR: Then why didn't you tell me right away?

TOPKNOT: Because he kept pinching and prodding me when I wanted to tell you. And when I wanted to let you get up, he kept pinching and prodding me too.

CASPAR: What a fresh little devil! I'm going to give you a crack on your fresh little horns!

LAZY DEVIL: Yah-boo! Can't catch me! Can't catch me!

CASPAR: Yes, I can! (*He tries to catch the little devil, who whizzes past him, back and forth.*)

LAZY DEVIL: Can't catch me! Can't catch me! And can't get rid of me either!

BROOM (*Dancing excitedly*):   Come and get me, Caspar! He fears me like fire and ice!

CASPAR (*Picking up the broom and chasing the little devil with it*):   Yes, this is the way! (*At last he hits the lazy devil, who flies off in a high arc.*)

TOPKNOT: Well done, Caspar! Well done, Broom!

CASPAR: So you're pleased now! Before you didn't want to let go of me.

TOPKNOT: It was only because he was pinching and prodding me. Now it's all over.

CASPAR: So now I can get on with the sweeping and cleaning, so that everything's spick-and-span before Grandma comes back.

TOPKNOT: Yes, sweep and clean now, and then Grandma will let you sleep late tomorrow.

CASPAR: And my friend Topknot, too, I suppose!

TOPKNOT: Your best of all friends!

BROOM: So long as the lazy devil doesn't creep back and pinch you again.

CASPAR: I'll tell you what . . . we'll put the broom by the bed. He fears the broom like fire and ice.

BROOM (*Dancing happily*): Like fire and ice! Like fire and ice!

CASPAR: Did you hear that, children?

CHILDREN: Yes!

CASPAR: If you have a friend like Topknot, give him my love. But tell him to watch out that Bones-ebub, the lazy devil, doesn't get him too. Good-bye for now, children.

Translated from the German by Joyce Emerson

Valentine

Tomorrow is Saint Valentine's day,
All in the morning betime,
And I a maid at your window,
To be your Valentine.

20

by William Shakespeare
Illustration by Cyndy Szekeres

Robinson Crusoe
by Charles E. Carryl

The night was thick and hazy
When the "Piccadilly Daisy"
Carried down the crew and captain in the sea;
   And I think the water drowned 'em,
   For they never, never found 'em,
And I know they didn't come ashore with me.

Oh! 'twas very sad and lonely
When I found myself the only
Population on this cultivated shore;
   But I've made a little tavern
   In a rocky little cavern,
And I sit and watch for people at the door.

I spent no time in looking
For someone to do my cooking,
As I'm quite a clever hand at making stews;
   But I had that fellow Friday,
   Just to keep the tavern tidy,
And to put a Sunday polish on my shoes.

21

OUR ENGLISH FRIEND
FRITZ WEGNER
ILLUSTRATED THIS
SILLY POEM, MUFFIN!

I DONT THINK I LIKE
THE PART ABOUT
BEETLE PIE!

I have a little garden
That I'm cultivating lard in,
As the things I eat are rather tough and dry;
For I live on toasted lizards,
Prickly pears, and parrot gizzards,
And I'm really very fond of beetle-pie.

The clothes I had were furry,
And it made me fret and worry
When I found the moths were eating off the hair;
And I had to scrape and sand 'em,
And I boiled 'em and I tanned 'em,
Till I got the fine morocco suit I wear.

22

"MOROCCO" IS A
KIND OF THIN, SOFT
LEATHER MADE OF
GOATSKIN

I sometimes seek diversion
In a family excursion
With the few domestic animals you see;
And we take along a carrot
As refreshment for the Parrot,
And a little can of jungleberry tea.

Then we gather, as we travel,
Bits of moss and dirty gravel,
And we chip off little specimens of stone;
And we carry home as prizes
Funny bugs, of handy sizes,
Just to give the day a scientific tone.

If the roads are wet and muddy,
We remain at home and study—
For the Goat is very clever at a sum—
And the Dog, instead of fighting,
Studies ornamental writing,
While the Cat is taking lessons on the drum.

We retire at eleven,
And we rise again at seven;
And I wish to call attention, as I close,
To the fact that all the scholars
Are correct about their collars,
And particular in turning out their toes.

Johnny Crow's Garden
by L. Leslie Brooke

Johnny Crow
Would dig and sow
Till he made a little garden.

And the lion
Had a green and yellow tie on
In Johnny Crow's garden.

And the rat
Wore a feather in his hat

26

But the bear
Had nothing to wear
In Johnny Crow's garden.

So the ape
Took his measure with a tape

In Johnny Crow's garden.

And the pig
Danced a jig
In Johnny Crow's garden.

And the whale
Told a very long tale
In Johnny Crow's garden.

And the fox
Put them all in the stocks
In Johnny Crow's garden.

32

But Johnny Crow
He let them go

And they all sat down
   to their dinner in a row
In Johnny Crow's garden.

The Neat Raccoon and the Untidy Owl

by Natalie Savage Carlson

accoons are neat, but Ronald was the neatest of them all. He lived by himself in an old oak tree in the woods. He always washed his paws and his food before he ate. He never carried any of his food back to his den because he liked to keep it neat, too. He left the fishbones and shrimp shells out on the bank of the creek.

"My home is neat as a mouse's tail and clean as a daisy," he liked to boast.

Although Ronald lived quite comfortably, he was very lonely.

"I wish I had someone to share my neat, clean house," he said to himself, since he had no one else to say it to. "Perhaps I should find a mate. Any wife would be happy with such a neat, clean husband."

He set out for the swamp where a pretty young raccoon lady lived.

"I'm very lonely all by myself," Ronald told her. "Will you marry me and come live in my house, which is neat as a mouse's tail and clean as a daisy?"

35

HI MUFFIN! *Cyndy Szekeres* DREW THESE NEAT, SWEET ILLUSTRATIONS...

I THINK I'VE FALLEN IN LOVE WITH RONALD!

OH No!

"I'm sorry," said the young raccoon, "but I'm already engaged to that big handsome raccoon who lives across the swamp. If you're lonely, come to my wedding."

Ronald went on his way. Oh, well, there were other raccoon ladies. He would try the one who lived in the piney woods.

He found her holding paws with a raccoon gentleman. So he only said, "Good evening! It looks as if it won't rain tonight," and turned away.

He was so discouraged that he decided to return home. He was halfway there when he came upon a big forlorn owl perched on a pine stump.

"I've never seen you here before," said Ronald.

"Who-o-o!" hooted the owl.

"You," answered Ronald. "Why are you sitting all alone on that stump?"

The owl looked even more forlorn. "I'm Oscar from across the freeway," he said, "but they cut down a lot of trees for a filling station. Mine was one of them. Now I have no home."

Ronald was sorry for the homeless owl. "Then won't you come and live with me?" he invited. "I'm all alone, too, but I live in a cozy home neat as a mouse's tail and clean as a daisy."

"Who-o-o!" hooted the owl.

"Me," answered Ronald. "I'm the neatest, cleanest raccoon in the whole country."

Oscar was only too happy to move into the oak tree with Ronald. The raccoon in turn was happy to have a companion. He wasn't lonely anymore. He didn't even bother going to the pretty young raccoon's wedding.

But soon Ronald began to wish he had never invited Oscar to share his home.

"Somebody has dirty nails," he accused.

"Who-o-o!" hooted Oscar.

"You," answered Ronald. "You look germy to me. Don't you ever wash your claws?"

"No need," said Oscar. "They're just as sharp for catching mice and frogs when they're dirty."

"Somebody is dragging chicken bones and mouse skins and eggshells into this house," accused Ronald.

"Who-o-o!" hooted Oscar.

"You," answered Ronald.

"Have to throw them somewhere," said Oscar. "They give me indigestion if I eat them."

37

At last Ronald couldn't stand Oscar's untidiness any longer. He decided to move out and leave the owl to live alone in his mess.

He explored the bank of the creek and found a hole recently left by a pair of otters. Then he was so hungry that he caught a shrimp. He washed it well although it had just come from the water. He tossed its shell over his shoulder. Finally, he went back to get his things and tell Oscar of his plans.

"I can't live in this house any longer," said Ronald. "I can't live with such an untidy roommate who drags bones and skins and shells into the house."

"Who-o-o!" hooted Oscar.

"You," answered Ronald. "We can't live together any longer. I've found a new home on the bank of the creek. I'm moving into it right away."

"It will be lonely without you," said Oscar. "Maybe I could try to keep my claws cleaner and not make such a mess in the house. But if you insist on leaving, I'll help you move."

They carried Ronald's grass bed out of the hole in the oak tree and down to the creek. Oscar looked all over the bank.

"It looks as if a crowd of human creatures had a picnic here," he said. "Look at all these fishbones and shells somebody has scattered over the bank."

"Who?" asked Ronald.

"You-ou-ou!" hooted Oscar.

"But what can I do with all the leavings?" asked Ronald. "I can't have them in my house, which will be neat as a mouse's tail and clean as a daisy."

Oscar scratched his tufted ear. "That's quite true," he agreed. "If we could think of a way to make our messes disappear, I'd be willing to help keep the house tidy and clean."

They sat down on the bank. They thought and thought.

At last Ronald knew what to do. "I have it!" he exclaimed. "That otter hole I was going to move into. We can throw all our messes into it."

"Who-o-o!" hooted Oscar.

"You and me," answered Ronald. "You clean out the hole in the oak tree, and I'll clean up this mess on the bank. Then we'll move back together."

Oscar went to clean up his mess. Ronald stayed on the bank to clean his. They dumped everything into the old otter hole.

At last they were finished. They stood paw to claw and looked at the bank of the creek.

"It must have looked like this a hundred years ago," said Ronald proudly.

"Who-o-o!" hooted Oscar.

"The creek," answered Ronald.

They carried the grass bed back into the tidy hole in the oak tree.

"Now our home is neat as a mouse's tail and clean as a daisy again," said Ronald. "And so is the bank of the creek. We make a good pair after all."

"Who-o-o!" hooted Oscar.

"You and me," answered Ronald. "We shall live happily ever after."

"After what?" asked Oscar.

"After we wash our paws and claws," answered Ronald. "That was dirty work."

Meet Your Author

Natalie Savage Carlson

It has been a long time since I was a child, but I remember my childhood clearly because it was a busy, happy one. I lived with my parents and three half-sisters and three whole sisters on a farm on the Potomac River in western Maryland.

My older half-sisters went away to boarding school, but a younger sister and I were taught by a young woman who lived in the village nearby. We were her only pupils, and we rode to her house on horseback. Since we were in school only in the morning, I had all afternoon to ride horseback and wander through the fields and woods. I have told about this in my book *The Half Sisters.*

My sisters and I liked to keep autograph books in which we had each other and our friends list their favorite things. Mine were these:

Favorite animal: Muskrat. I wanted to catch a baby muskrat at our pond and raise it as a pet.

Favorite bird: Mourning dove. They nested in our peach orchard. I brought a pair of little ones home to raise as pets with my pigeons, but I had taken them from the nest too early so they died.

Favorite book: *Wild Animals I Have Known* by Ernest Thompson Seton. Since I lived on a farm, I knew many wild animals myself. But I liked the muskrats best.

Favorite sport: Horseback riding.

Favorite hobby: Writing stories. I have had twenty-six books published, but I also like to write short stories like "The Neat Raccoon and the Untidy Owl."

OF SHIPS AND TREES

by Beatrice Tanaka

When someone comes home after a long trip, the villagers who have never traveled farther than the neighboring market always listen wide-eyed to the traveler's tales. It is an invitation to brag, and some returning travelers just can't resist the temptation.

One young man, back from a long journey, once told his admiring audience a new story every evening—each story stranger and more wonderful than the last.

"I once saw a ship in a foreign port," he said one evening, "and it was sooooo enormous you couldn't even imagine its size if you tried! Why, a young boy who set out from the prow would arrive at the stern an old, white-haired man."

"Oooooooh!" gasped the audience.

"What is so wonderful about that?" asked a woodcutter, who was getting annoyed with these nightly bragging sessions. "In the forest not far from here, I once saw some trees so huge, sooo old, sooooo tall, that a bird that had been flying for ten years hadn't even reached halfway to the top."

"Liar!" cried the traveler. "Trees like that don't exist."

The woodcutter smiled. "Then where do you suppose the carpenters found the wood for your ship's mast?" he asked.

A Folk Tale from Vietnam

Nautical knots by Martha Lehtola

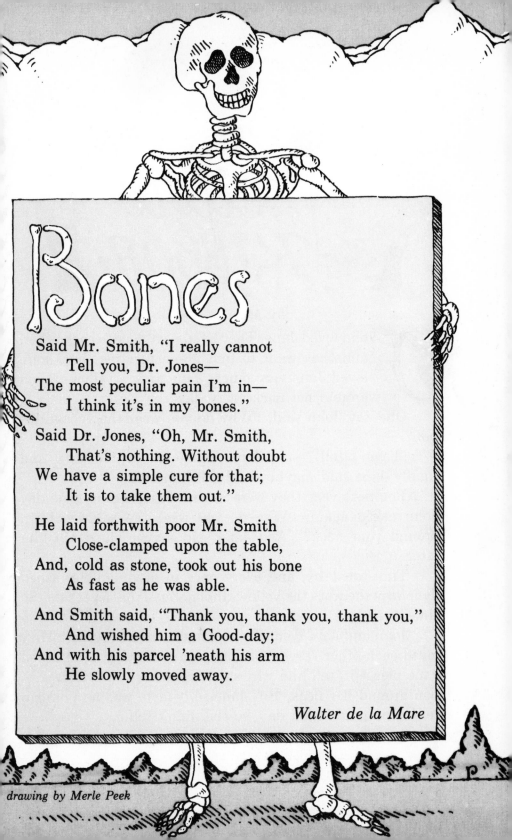

Bones

Said Mr. Smith, "I really cannot
  Tell you, Dr. Jones—
The most peculiar pain I'm in—
  I think it's in my bones."

Said Dr. Jones, "Oh, Mr. Smith,
  That's nothing. Without doubt
We have a simple cure for that;
  It is to take them out."

He laid forthwith poor Mr. Smith
  Close-clamped upon the table,
And, cold as stone, took out his bone
  As fast as he was able.

And Smith said, "Thank you, thank you, thank you,"
  And wished him a Good-day;
And with his parcel 'neath his arm
  He slowly moved away.

Walter de la Mare

drawing by Merle Peek

The Yellow Ribbon

by Maria Leach

John loved Jane. They lived next door to each other, and they went to first grade together, and John loved Jane very much. Jane wore a yellow ribbon around her neck every day.

One day John said, "Why do you wear the yellow ribbon?"

"I can't tell," said Jane. But John kept asking, and finally Jane said maybe she'd tell him later.

The next year they were in the second grade. One day John asked again, "Why do you wear the yellow ribbon around your neck?" And Jane said maybe she'd tell him later.

Time went by, and every once in a while John asked Jane why she wore the yellow ribbon, but Jane never told. So time went by.

John and Jane went through high school together. They loved each other very much. On graduation day John asked Jane please to tell him why she always wore the yellow ribbon around her neck. But Jane said there was no point in telling on graduation day, so she didn't tell.

Illustrations by Trina Schart Hyman

Time went by, and John and Jane became engaged, and finally Jane said maybe she would tell him on their wedding day.

The wedding day came, and John forgot to ask. But the next day John asked Jane why she wore the yellow ribbon. Jane said, "Well, we are happily married, and we love each other, so what difference does it make?" So John let it pass, but he still *did* want to know.

Time went by, and finally on their golden anniversary John asked again. And Jane said, "Since you have waited this long, you can wait a little longer."

Finally Jane was taken very ill, and when she was dying John asked again, between sobs, "*Please* tell me why you wear the yellow ribbon around your neck."

"All right," said Jane, "you can untie it."

So John untied the yellow ribbon, and Jane's head fell off.

OH NO!
GROSS!

Cricket's Critter Cottage

by Elaine Livermore

2 dogs, 2 birds, 2 mice, 2 cats, 2 rabbits, and 2 snakes are hiding in Cricket's Critter Cottage. Can you find them?

ALFRED
AND THE FIERCE,
FIERY FOX BY
HELEN CRESSWELL

Once upon a time—yesterday, was it?—there was a boy called Alfred who didn't believe in things. He didn't believe in dragons, for instance, or witches, or magic lamps—he didn't believe in *anything*, Alfred didn't. He was in great danger of growing up to be impossibly dull and boring, when one day something happened to change his mind. It not only changed his mind; it changed Alfred.

Alfred lived in the town. He lived in an apartment fourteen stories up. This meant that he lived in two worlds. He lived in a high "I'm the king of the castle" world, where he looked down on things from way up high like a bird or a man on very long stilts. Instead of houses, he saw roofs; instead of people, he saw hats; and when the moon came up at night, he felt it was so near that he could almost touch it, or talk to it. (Not that he believed in the man in the moon, of course.)

Illustrated by fiery Friso Henstra

The other world, the one he saw when he went down in the elevator with his mother, was very different. Instead of looking down, he had to look up. In fact, every day of his life he found himself being surprised at how big people really were.

Each night when he lay in bed, Alfred's mother sang a song to him. And one particular night she sang a song from a picture book she had brought from the library:

The fox went out on a chilly night,
Prayed for the moon to give him light;
He had many a mile to go that night
Before he reached the town-o.

She sang it all the way through, and Alfred listened. He heard how the fox came to the town to hunt and how the farmer fetched his gun, but the fox stole the goose and ran back to his den, and there

The fox and his wife without any strife
Cut up the goose with a carving knife.
They never had such a supper in their life,
And the little ones chewed on the bones-o.

"What's a fox?" Alfred asked when the song was finished. "What's a fox *look* like?" because he liked the *sound* of the fox very much indeed. A fine, bold, splendid fellow he seemed to Alfred.

"Here," said Alfred's mother, "I'll show you."

She began to sing the song again, and this time she showed him the book at the same time, turning the pages slowly one by one.

And for the first time in his whole life Alfred saw what a fox looked like. He saw a creature fiery red and fierce, leaping across the pages with lolling tongue and greedy eye. And that fox, with his family of little foxes hidden away in his secret den, was the most beautiful, wicked, magic thing Alfred had ever known.

"Again!" he cried when his mother had finished the song. "Again!"

"Not now," she said, and closed the book.

Alfred opened his mouth to scream. He found that just opening his mouth usually worked. His actual scream was very loud indeed. Ear-splitting, in fact. It worked tonight. His mother sang the song again, and again Alfred looked at the pictures of the gay red fox leaping through the moonlight.

When it was over, he said, "*We* live in the town-o. It says in the song that the fox went to the town-o."

"Yes, but not this town, dear," said his mother. "Don't worry—there are no foxes in this town."

"There is," said Alfred. "There *is*."

"No, dear," said his mother. "I promise you."

"There is, there is, there is!" said Alfred. He wanted above all things for there to be a fierce, fiery fox hunting through the moonlight in *his* town, past his very window.

"All right, dear," said his mother. "There is. Now, go to sleep."

She put out the light.

"And the little ones chewed on the bones-o," said Alfred lovingly. "They must have had big *teeth,* even if they were little."

"That's right. Good night, dear."

And she went out, leaving the door open so that a band of light came in from the hall and lit up Alfred's fort on the chest of drawers.

"There *is* a fox in this town-o," said Alfred to himself.

So sure was he of this, that after a minute or so he crawled from under the tightly tucked blankets, opened the curtain, and kneeling on the bed, looked out.

The lights of the town lay below him. Then there was a band of dark, and then the moon, on a level with Alfred himself, or so it seemed.

"The moon is over the town-o!" muttered Alfred under his breath. "Now for the fox-o! Come quickly, fox, come quick!"

And as he stared into the pattern of familiar lights, he grew so hungry, so ravenous, for the sight of a fox with red plumy tail, that he knew he must see him that very night. And he stared and stared so hard that when the fox *did* come, it was as if Alfred had *made* him come.

The fox was so beautiful, so fierce and fiery, and he leaped so silently out of the stars that Alfred banged his fists on the windowsill with unbearable excitement. And the fox was bigger than the fox on the pages had been, bigger, more shining russet, more marvelous in every way.

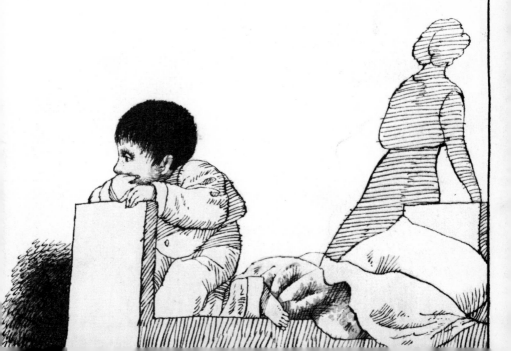

He strode through the sky with the moonlight on his back tipping each separate hair with a cold, blinding fire. And down he stepped, always down, till he reached the roofs and chimneys of the town below. And there he hunted under Alfred's worshipping gaze. He leaped from house to house, stepping light on roofs under which people slept or talked or watched television. And none of them knew or even dreamed that the fox was so near, snuffling and searching over their very heads. A wild, greedy, untamed fox had come to the town and was stamping it under his feet. Hither and thither he ran and bent his head and sniffed.

"The goose!" called Alfred. "Where's the goose?"

And no sooner had he spoken than the geese were there, too. It was as if they had been made out of his words.

A gaggle of geese stormed over the rooftops. Alfred did not hear them, but he saw them go into a whirlwind, like a catherine-wheel of white wings and stiffened necks. And they too were bigger and whiter and more gloriously fat and panicky than the goose Alfred had seen in the pages of the book.

The fox stopped. Stockstill he stood on a steep roof. Then he lifted his head. The fur on his back stood stiff and separate; the moon struck sparks along it right to the tip of his brush.

Then he sprang.

"Quick, fox, quick!" called Alfred.

The geese scattered and the fox picked one, just one, and the chase was on. Fox and goose went vaulting then, mad and quick, the goose frantic and the fox bent to kill. And Alfred, drumming his fists on the windowsill, was willing them both to win, wanting the goose to go free *and* the fox to kill. But it was the fox he watched, his own fierce, fiery fox, and he knew what the end of the chase must be. Part of

him wanted the goose to go flapping free and hide among the chimney stacks and keep there safe till dawn when the fox must go. But he thought of the little ones—eight, nine, ten—ten red foxes waiting supperless in their secret den among the stars.

"Get him, fox!" he shouted. "Quick, get him!"

Because he could not bear to watch any longer, he shut his eyes, and when he opened them, the goose was dangling in the fox's mouth, and the fox was heading home.

"Oh goose, poor goose!" and Alfred rubbed his eyes with his fists. But he saw the blurred red fire that was his fox leap

smoothly back into the air and start his journey home, and
Alfred was proud of him, and glad. The fox had hunted well
that night in the town-o, and had deserved his prize. He was
back among the stars now, growing smaller every minute.
Soon he would be in his den. Alfred pictured his little ones:
eight, nine, ten, and could almost hear them cry,

> *Daddy, better go back again*
> *For it must be a mighty fine town-o!*

And he knew in his heart of hearts that there were as
many geese left as he, Alfred, wanted there to be. That the
fierce, fiery fox could have a goose every night of his life, if
only he came to Alfred's town-o.

The fox was only a red spark now. Alfred let the curtain
drop. He got back into bed and lay still, seeing again the
blazing trail of the fox among the chimneys. He decided not
to tell his mother.

"She wouldn't believe it," he thought.

But Alfred did. For once you can make your own foxes,
you have to believe in them. And there is a fox waiting to be
made in every town-o. Just waiting . . . .

THE FOX

O the fox went out on a chilly night,
Prayed for the moon to give him light; He had many a mile to
go that night Be- fore he reached the town-o,
town-o, town-o, Many a mile to

Em   A7   Dm7   G7   C

go that night Be- fore he reached the town-o.

Well, he ran 'til he came to a great big pen,
Where the ducks and the geese were kept therein.
"A couple o' you gonna grease my chin
Before I leave this town-o, town-o, town-o,
A couple o' you gonna grease my chin
Before I leave this town-o."

He grabbed the gray goose by the neck,
Throwed a duck across his back;
He didn't mind the quack, quack, quack,
And their legs all dangling down-o, down-o, down-o,
He didn't mind the quack, quack, quack,
And their legs all dangling down-o.

Old mother Flipper Flopper jumped out of bed,
Out of the window she stuck her head,
Crying, "John, John, the gray goose is gone,
And the fox is on the town-o, town-o, town-o,
John, John, the gray goose is gone,
And the fox is on the town-o."

The fox he ran to his own wee den,
There were the little ones eight, nine, ten,
Crying, "Daddy, better go back again
'Cause it must be a mighty fine town-o, town-o, town-o,
Daddy, better go back again
'Cause it must be a mighty fine town-o."

Then the fox and his wife without any strife,
Cut up the goose with a carving knife;
They never had such a supper in their life,
And the little ones chewed on the bones-o, bones-o, bones-o,
They never had such a supper in their life,
And the little ones chewed on the bones-o.

Old Cricket says

If your neighbor called you "silly," I don't think you'd like it very much. But, hundreds of years ago it meant "happy, lucky, blessed." And "neighbor" meant "a nearby farmer." Boys used to be called "girls." "Lord" meant "bread-keeper," and "lady" was a woman who kneaded bread. Words grow and change just as we do. They're part of our history, and if you look behind words you'll see ancient Greeks and Romans, Anglo-Saxons, Vikings, Africans, Arabians, Indians—just about the whole world.

Have some fun, next time you look up a word in the dictionary. See where it comes from; not only what it means now, but what it used to mean. How about "bonfire"? Or "curfew"? Or "handkerchief"? You'll be surprised.

Once in a while, a story may have a few words you haven't met before. You can probably guess what they mean. Even so, it's an adventure to explore them in the dictionary. There, if you're curious, one word can put you on the trail of another, and you'll come across a dozen things you never expected.

Do you know the tale of Ali Baba and the magic words "Open, sesame!" that let him enter the cave of treasure? Our language is one of our greatest treasures, and we don't need magic words to find it. Just open the dictionary. (By the way, do you know what "sesame" is? Look it up!)

Old Cricket

SPLINTER

by Carl Sandburg

The voice of the last cricket
across the first frost
is one kind of good-by.
It is so thin a splinter of singing.

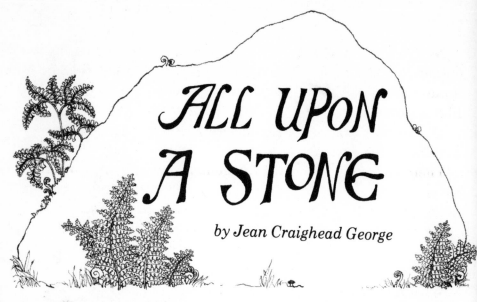

ALL UPON A STONE

by *Jean Craighead George*

In the woods by a stream lies an old worn stone. It is big as a bear and gray as a rain cloud.

Moss gardens grow on its ridges and humps. Ferns cast shadows of lace on its sides. A puddle of water lies like a lake near its top and butterflies sit nearby.

A stone by a stream in the woods is like a tiny country. It has its own forests, valleys, and pools. It has its own creatures that live out their lives, hunting, sleeping, and working all upon a stone.

A summer day dawns.

Deep under the stone a mole cricket moves.

Fuzzy hairs cover his back like fur. His feet are small shovels that dig the soil as he hunts for food.

As he works by himself in the ground under the stone, he breathes through his belly. He hears with his knees, smells with his antennae, and sees through the thousands of parts of his eyes.

Since his hatching in spring his knees have never heard another mole cricket. His antennae have never smelled one.

60

This is a story about my cousin!

Is he as funny-looking as you are?

Nancie Swanberg did the drawings. She's a friend of mine!

Now on this summer day his antennae stretched as he sniffed for the scent of another mole cricket. He peered around roots looking for furry backs, shovels, and knees just like his own.

Tunneling as he searched, he worked himself up to the bottom of the stone.

There he came to a sowbug. He gently touched her with his antenna, but she was no mole cricket. She tucked down her head, pulled in her feet, and rolled herself into a ball.

He crept a little farther, lifting his knees to listen for the crackles of a mole cricket.

He met a ground beetle. She clicked. He went on.

With his shovels he dug up a salamander that was lying under the stone. Its back was not furry but slick and wet.

With his knees he listened to spiders, centipedes, and ants, but he heard no mole cricket crackles.

He tunneled to the surface and came up beside the edge of the stone.

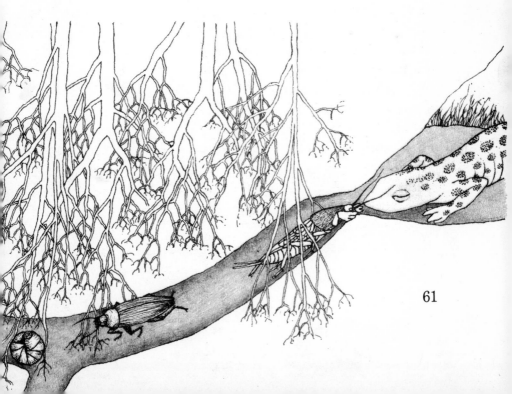

61

Thousands of sunbeams spun in his eyes. To shade them he pushed his head between his brown shovels. His two big eyes protected, he entered a path that led up through the moss that covered one side of the stone.

Slowly he climbed.

He heard silken slithers. He followed the sound through the moss. A wood snail was sliding on its big foot. A bright path of silver marked where it had walked.

The mole cricket hurried along.

Under a fern he paused for a rest. A pleasant odor came down his antennae.

He peered through the thousands of parts of his eyes. It was only a firefly asleep in the fern fronds waiting for twilight, his hour to fly and to glow.

The cricket stepped along with all his six feet.

At the edge of a pit filled with stone dust he listened again.

He heard crashes, not crackles. Worker ants were stacking sand grains on sand grains. The sound was enormous.

At last he came to the pool in the stone. It smelled like a mole cricket.

He grew excited. He fell in. Plowing the water of the rock pool as if it were soil, he swam.

And as he swam he passed fairy shrimp. They darted away upside down for they live on their backs.

Young mosquitoes flipped to the bottom of the pool. His shovels struck algae and rotifers and freshwater jellyfish. He bumped the tip of a freshwater sponge.

But he did not find a mole cricket.

He beached in a grove of bright bluets and dried off his fur with his second pair of legs.

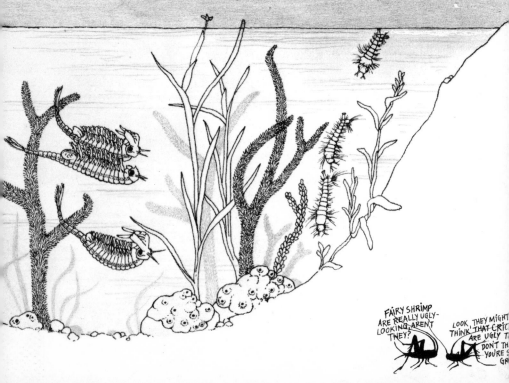

FAIRY SHRIMP ARE REALLY UGLY-LOOKING, AREN'T THEY?

LOOK, THEY MIGHT THINK THAT CRIC ARE UGLY T DON'T TH E YOU'RE S G

Silver wings flashed. The mole cricket lifted his knees. The clatter of stone flies was all that he heard. They had hatched in the stream by the stone and were dancing above the bluet grove.

He wedged himself under a starflower. A ground spider leaped to a leaf to pounce on him. He scurried away.

Then in a jungle of liverwort plants the tap of his shovels on dry leaves and stone awakened a lizard. He sprang at the cricket. Terrified, the cricket dug himself into a hump of pincushion moss.

The lizard was baffled. He went back to his lair.

The mole cricket continued to dig, and soon came out in

the sun. He saw that he had come to the top of the stone. It was scattered with lichens and smoothed by the rain.

He listened and looked.

No mole cricket crackles came to his knees. No furry backs glowed in the thousands of parts of his eyes.

He set up a wail. Locking one wing into the other, he sawed out his cry.

He crackled. He crackled his loneliness. He crackled his whereabouts. He crackled his need for other mole crickets.

Down on the stone dropped a single mole cricket. Speeding around trees came another. Up from the bank of the stream flew a third and a fourth, a fifth and a sixth and a seventh.

They gathered together as mole crickets do, not to mate, not to eat, but for reasons no one knows. Solitary creatures all the days of their lives, each leaves his earthen home on one festive night and rushes together with other mole crickets to dance, crackle, and touch.

The mole cricket joined them. His knees heard glorious crackles. He smelled the good scent of other mole crickets. He saw furry backs.

He mingled and met. He bumped, touched, and scrambled. He sang, whirled, and crackled. He danced all night to mole cricket sounds.

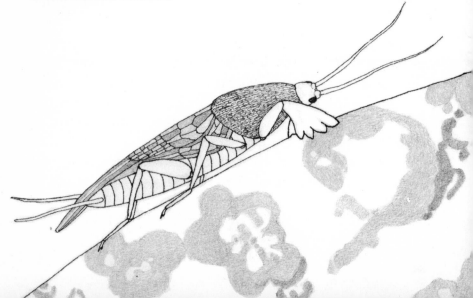

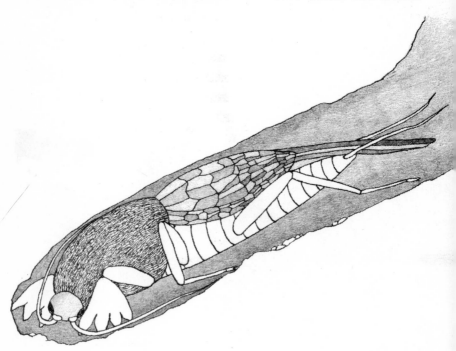

Then he sat still. He was weary. There were too many crackles, too many backs, too many knees, and too many eyes.

Wildly he flew from the stone. He crashed into other crickets flying away.

He zoomed to the ground and plunged into the loam. He tunneled and burrowed and scrambled toward silence. He dug away from the sight of mole cricket fur. He raced from the scent of their bodies.

He plowed to a quiet spot under the stone.

His senses now told him that he loved his mole cricket comforts deep in the earth, the silence, the darkness, the black hugging soil.

Back in his home he sighed through his belly, pulled down his antennae, and stretched out to rest under the stone.

A Boy
Named

 by William Cole

Once there was a little boy—
His name was Mary Jane—
Who lived 'way down in a tiny town
Called Washington, in Spain;
Whenever he went walking
He took his dog and cat;
His kitty's name was "Rover";
He called his doggie "Scat"!
  Is there anything wrong with that?

69

Lloyd Alexander drew these funny pictures

His mother was a plumber
With a heavy bag of tools;
His father taught crocheting
In all the local schools;
His sister was a boxer,
(Her given name was Paul.)
But Mary Jane himself had not
One single job at all.
    (Because he was too small.)

The summer he was two years old,
Or maybe in his teens,
His father went to Iceland
To buy some tangerines;
His mother went to Scotland
To play some basketball;
But Mary Jane he stayed at home—
He *still* was much too small—
    Till they returned next fall.

One day he said to Poppa,
"I don't know who's to blame,
But Holy Moses! Goodness sake!
I do not like my *name!*"
His poppa said, "Now, Janey,
If two noble deeds you'll do
We'll think about another name
More suitable to you—
    Like maybe 'Kalamazoo'?"

So Jane went to the forest
And came upon a fish
Who'd tripped upon some seaweed.
(He heard it mutter, "Pish!")
It had a swollen ankle;
Jane fixed it with some string;
The fish hopped happily away
Waving with his wing.
    A most peculiar thing!

Then next week, in the ocean,
He came upon a cat
Who'd been out pleasure-swimming
And got bitten by a bat.
Jane soothed the wound with butter,
(You'll find lots undersea.)
And pussy was quite grateful:
"What noble deedery!"
  And Jane said, "Huh? Who *me?*"

And so he ran to Poppa,
And said, "Hey, listen, Dad—
Two noble deeds I've gone and did."
His poppa said, "Good lad—
I always knew you had the stuff;
Come shake my horny mitt;
I'll change your name to 'Oshkosh,' "
And Jane said, "Gosh! That's it!
  A really perfect fit!"

They all were very happy;
And I've got this to say:
Boys! If *you'd* be happy
You *must* learn to crochet!
And girls—you take up plumbing;
It's work that leads to fame;
And if you chance to have a son,
Don't cause him any shame—
     Let Oshkosh be his name!

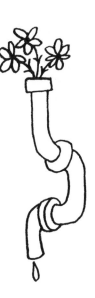

ISN'T THAT SILLY?
WHO EVER HEARD
OF A BOY NAMED
MARY JANE?

CRICKET, I NEVER
TOLD YOU BEFORE
BUT MY MIDDLE NAME
IS MARVIN!

THAT'S OKAY—
MY MIDDLE NAME
IS VICTORIA ELIZABETH!

⚙he ⚙nail's ⚙onologue

by Christian Morgenstern

Shall I dwell in my shell?
Shall I not dwell in my shell?
Dwell in shell?
Rather not dwell?
Shall I not dwell,
shall I dwell,
dwell in shell,
shall I shell,
shallIshellIshallIshellIshallI . . . ?

IN CASE YOU DIDN'T KNOW,
"MONOLOGUE" MEANS A SPEECH
BY ONE PERSON ! IT'S FROM
THE GREEK WORDS "MONO"— WHICH
MEANS "ONE", AND "LOGUE" WHICH
MEANS "SPEAKING." (A DIALOGUE
IS A SPEECH FOR TWO
PEOPLE !)

CRICKE
SURE AF
AT MO

(The snail gets so entangled with his thoughts or, rather, the
thoughts run away with him so that he must postpone the
decision.)

Translated from the German by Max Knight

SLUGGO, JUDITH LERNER DID THE DRAWING FOR THIS POEM DO YOU LIKE IT?

I'M TOO EMBARASSED TO THINK ABOUT IT.

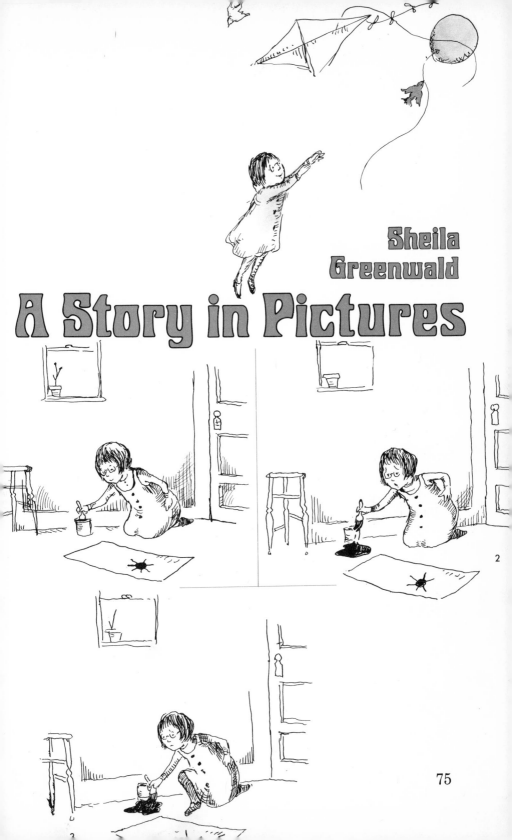

A Story in Pictures

Sheila Greenwald

2

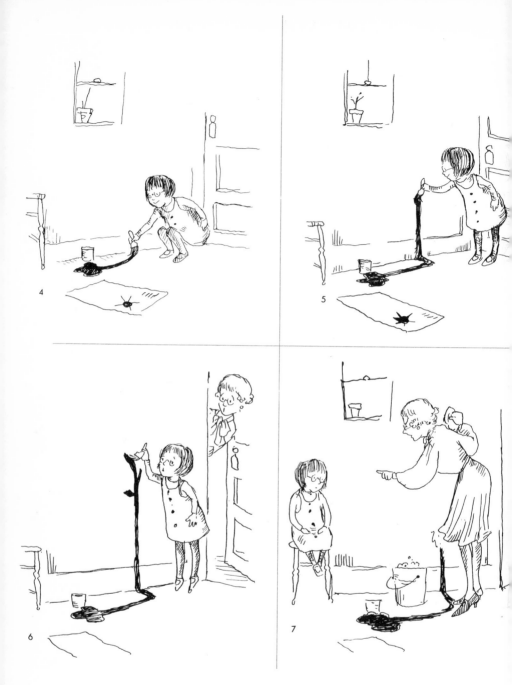

4

5

6

7

76

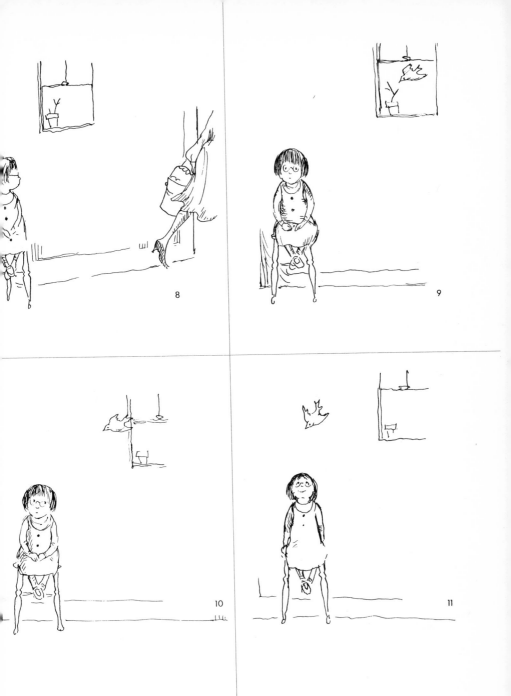

8

9

10

11

12

15

14

16

17

18

19

79

20

21

22

80

25

26

27

28

29

30

31

82

My Sister Laura
Spike Milligan

My sister Laura's bigger than me
And lifts me up quite easily.
I can't lift her—I've tried and tried;
She must have something heavy inside.

Cheese Please

by Paul Galdone

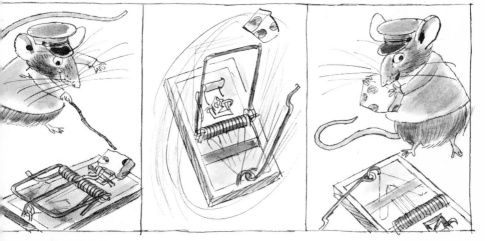

A Thousand Years Ago
by Clifton Fadiman

People believed, a thousand years ago,
In lots of things that weren't really so.

There's never *been* a DRAGON, wild *or* tame,
But they were scared of dragons all the same,
Scared of his pointed tail, his dreadful claws,
His batlike wings, and fire-breathing jaws.

Illustrated by the inimitable Wallace Tripp.

Another beast no one has ever seen
On any road, in any forest green,
Was something like a horse, had one long horn,
And swished a lion's tail: the UNICORN.

And still another about which I've read
Had but to look at you—and you were dead!
It seems to me you ran an awful risk
If you got friendly with a BASILISK!

The GRIFFIN had an eagle's head and wings,
A body like a lion. These queer things
You'll find inside a picture book—but you
Will never, *never* find them in a zoo!

People believed, a thousand years ago,
In lots of things that weren't really so.

87

HOW DOES <u>HE</u> KNOW?
I'LL BET THERE REALLY
WERE DRAGONS!

I LIKE
UNICORNS
BETTER.

by Lloyd Alexander

When Princess Angharad of the Royal House of Llyr came of an age to be married, her mother, Queen Regat, sent throughout the kingdom to find suitors for her daughter's hand. With red-gold hair and sea-green eyes, Angharad was the most beautiful of princesses, and many would have courted her. However, because Angharad was of an ancient family of enchantresses, it was forbidden her to wed any but an enchanter.

"That," said Angharad, "is the most ridiculous rule I've ever heard of. It's vexing enough, having to curtsy here, curtsy there, smile when you'd rather frown, frown when you'd rather laugh, and look interested when you're actually bored to tears. And now, is my husband to be chosen for me?"

"Rules are to be obeyed, not questioned," answered Queen Regat. "You may wed the one your heart desires, and choose your husband freely—among those, naturally, with suitable qualifications."

"It seems to me," said Angharad, "one of the qualifications should be that we love each other."

"Desirable," said Queen Regat, "but in matters of state, not always practical."

And so Queen Regat commanded that only enchanters of the highest skill should present themselves in turn at the Great Hall of the Castle of Llyr.

First came the enchanter Gildas. He was fat, with fleshy cheeks shining as if buttered. His garments were embroidered with gold thread and crusted with jewels. The servants following him were dressed almost as splendidly as their master, and murmurs of admiration rose from the assembled courtiers. Nose in the air, Gildas bustled through the Great Hall to stand before the thrones of Angharad and her mother.

"Noblest ladies," Gildas began, with a curt nod of his balding head, "only with greatest difficulty have I been able to spare a few moments from an especially busy morning. Therefore, I hope we may promptly settle the amount of treasure the Princess will bring me as her marriage portion."

"What?" burst out Angharad, before her mother could reply. "Prompt settlement? Treasure? You're a good step ahead of yourself, Master Gildas. I'd first like to see some of your enchantments. Then I'll make up my own mind."

Sniffling impatiently, Gildas began mumbling and muttering, droning spells, waving his arms, and waggling his fingers. At last, a small gray cloud took shape in the air. Bigger and blacker it grew until it blotted out the sunlight from the windows and the Great Hall was dark as midnight. Then Gildas clapped his hands, the cloud drained away, and the Great Hall was bright as it had been before. The courtiers whispered in amazement. Princess Angharad stifled a yawn.

Trina Schart Hyman
DREW THE PICTURES

NO, SHE'S AGGRAVATING!

IS SHE ENCHANTING?

"Well?" she said.

Gildas blinked at her. "I beg your pardon?"

"Is that all there is to it?"

"All there is?" exclaimed Gildas. "One of my finest effects! My dear Princess—"

"My dear enchanter," Angharad replied, "frankly I don't see the point of going to such trouble to turn day into night. All anybody needs to do is be patient and night will come along very nicely by itself, with far better darkness than yours—much more velvety. Not to mention the moon and a whole skyful of stars for good measure."

"Then, Princess," returned Gildas, taken aback, "allow me to produce—a snowstorm? My blizzards never fail to please."

90

Angharad sighed and shrugged. "There again, Master Gildas, why bother? When the proper season comes 'round, we'll have snow enough; each flake different. Can you do as well?"

Sputtering and stammering, Gildas admitted he could not. "But—but, perhaps, a full-course feast? Roast goose? Wine? Sweetmeats?"

"We're quite satisfied with our own cook," said Angharad. "Thank you, no."

Scowling in wounded dignity, Gildas seated himself beside Queen Regat, awaiting the next suitor.

Now came the enchanter Grimgower. He was lean, thin-faced, with knotted brows and a square black beard twining around his lips. His iron-shod boots rang and his black cloak streamed behind him as he strode toward the thrones. Dark-robed, hooded servants marched after him, and the courtiers drew back uneasily as they passed.

Grimgower halted before Angharad, folded his arms, and threw back his head.

"Princess," he said, "I come to claim your hand and declare myself willing to accept you as my wife."

"At least," replied Angharad, "that settles half the question."

"Let us understand each other," said Grimgower. "No luxury will be denied you. You shall have all you wish, and more. But in my household, I am the only master."

"You make it sound delightful," said Angharad. "You've shown me the sort of husband you'd be. Would you mind showing me what sort of enchanter you are?"

Grimgower stepped back a pace and raised his arms. In a harsh voice he called out the words of a mighty spell. Suddenly, out of thin air, sprang monstrous creatures that

91

OH BOY, NOW I'M REALLY SCARED!

snarled, bared sharp fangs, and snapped their jaws. Some, covered with scales, breathed fire through their nostrils; others lashed tails as sharp as swords. The courtiers gasped in terror. Queen Regat paled and stiffened, but Angharad glanced calmly at the monsters.

"Poor things, they look starved for their dinner," she said to Grimgower. "You should really take better care of them. They need a good brushing and combing, too. I daresay they're all flea-ridden."

"These are no common enchantments," cried Grimgower, his face twisting angrily, "but creatures shaped of my own dreams. I alone can summon them. You shall not see their like in all the kingdom."

"Happily," said Angharad. "Yes, I suppose they would be the sort of things you, Master Grimgower, would dream of, and no doubt you're proud of them. I hope you won't be offended if I tell you honestly I prefer the animals we have in our forest. The deer are much handsomer than that dismal whatever-it-is next to you. So are the rabbits, the raccoons, and all the others. And I'm sure they have better tempers."

Frowning darkly, Grimgower spat a magic word through his teeth and the monstrous beings disappeared as quickly as they had come. Then the enchanter took his place beside Gildas and the two rivals looked daggers at each other.

"So far," Angharad whispered to her mother, "the choice is easy: Neither!"

"One more awaits," Queen Regat answered. "Geraint is his name. He is unknown to me, but he asks admittance to seek your hand."

Angharad shrugged and sighed wearily. "I've put up with these two. I doubt a third could be more tiresome."

But the Princess caught her breath as Geraint made his

93

way through the Great Hall and stood before her. He came with no servants; his garments were plain and unadorned. Yet this youth was the fairest she had ever seen. Nevertheless, despite her quickening heart and the color rising to her cheeks, she tossed her head and said lightly, "Now, Master Geraint, with what enchantments do you mean to court us?"

Geraint smiled as he replied, "Why, Princess, with none at all. Does a man court a woman with sorcery? It seems to me he must court her with love."

"Boldly spoken," said Angharad, "but how shall you do so?"

"As a man to a woman," answered Geraint. "And may you answer me freely, as a woman to a man."

As their eyes met, Angharad knew her heart could be given only to him. However, before she could reply, Gildas stepped forward, sputtering a protest; Grimgower sprang from his seat and angrily insisted that Geraint prove his skill, as they had been obliged to do.

And so Geraint began. He pronounced no magical spells but, instead, in common, quiet words he spoke of waters and woodlands, of sea and sky, of men and women, of childhood and old age, of the wonder and beauty of living things, all closely woven one with the other as threads on the same loom.

As he spoke, he stretched out his open hands, and all in the court fell silent, marveling. For now, born of his simple gesture, appeared flights of doves, fluttering and circling around him. Flowers blossomed at each motion of his fingers. He raised his arms and above his head stars glittered in a sparkling cloud and a shower of lights was scattered through the Great Hall.

Then Geraint lowered his arms to his sides, and the enchantments vanished. He stood waiting, saying nothing more, while his glance and the glance of Angharad touched and held each other. Smiling, the Princess rose from her throne.

"My choice is made," she said. "Geraint has sought my hand and won my heart. And so shall we be wed."

Shouts of joy filled the Great Hall as Angharad and Geraint stepped forward to embrace.

But Grimgower thrust himself between them. His face paled with rage as he cried out, "What trickery is this? He used no sorcery known to me or to any magician. He is a false enchanter! Cast him out!"

"He has tried to cheat us," fumed Gildas, his cheeks shaking with indignation. "I heard no proper spells or charms. This upstart has no true power. A mere juggler!"

Angharad was about to protest, but the Queen gestured for her to be silent.

"You have heard these accusations," Queen Regat said sternly to Geraint. "Are they true?"

"Yes," Geraint answered willingly, "altogether true. Sorcery is not my birthright. I have no inborn powers. What I showed, I fashioned by myself. The birds you saw? No doves, but only bits of white parchment. The flowers? Dry grass and tinted leaves. The stars? A handful of bright pebbles. I only helped you imagine these things to be more than what they are. If this pleased you for a few moments, I ask nothing better."

"How dare you come to us claiming to be an enchanter?" demanded the Queen.

"To win Angharad's hand," replied Geraint, "I would dare more than that."

"Even so," answered the Queen, "my daughter has chosen you in vain."

"No!" declared Angharad. "Any other choice would be in vain. These two inherited their skills. Geraint earned his. False? He's the only true enchanter!"

"Nevertheless," Queen Regat answered, "by rule and custom, your marriage to him is forbidden."

Since Angharad would consent to none but Geraint, the Queen regretfully commanded the Princess to withdraw and remain in her chambers. Geraint was sent from the Castle of Llyr.

But Angharad defied the ancient rule and followed Geraint, and found him waiting for her as if each had known the other's mind.

As the two made their way through the forest beyond the castle, suddenly the sky grew dark as midnight, though the day was barely past high noon. But, from her cloak, Angharad drew a golden sphere which glowed at her touch and whose light overcame this vengeful sorcery of Gildas.

Then, in front of Angharad and Geraint sprang monstrous creatures sent by Grimgower. But the two clasped hands and kept on their way. And the creatures drew back and bowed their heads while the lovers passed unharmed.

At the edge of the forest a thick curtain of snow began to fall, and icy winds lashed Angharad and Geraint. But they held each other closer and so passed through it, too, in warmth and safety.

And where they left footprints in the snow, flowers bloomed.

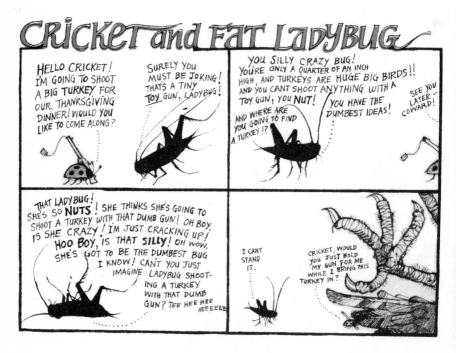

Lean Out of the Window

Lean out of the window,
   Goldenhair,
I heard you singing
   A merry air.

My book was closed;
   I read no more,
Watching the fire dance
   On the floor.

I have left my book,
   I have left my room,
For I heard you singing
   Through the gloom.

Singing and singing
   A merry air,
Lean out of the window,
   Goldenhair.

James Joyce

Drawing by Trina Schart Hyman

Mrs. Pepperpot and the Puppet Show

by Alf Prøysen

Mrs. Pepperpot is a funny old woman who at the oddest moments shrinks to the size of a pepperpot.

I t was a lovely summer's day, just the day for an outing. The village sewing club had been invited to a television show in the next town, and they were going by special bus.

Mrs. Pepperpot was going too, and she was very excited, because she had never watched a puppet show in a TV studio before. Nor had any of the others, for that matter. They had all put on their best summer dresses and straw hats with flowers.

When they got to the town, the bus stopped in the market-place and they all got off and filed into the theater. They felt rather shy when they were given the front row of seats, but soon they were all comfortably seated with little bags of peppermints to munch. All except Mrs. Pepperpot. Where was she?

Well, you know how she likes to poke her nose into things, and as they were walking down the aisle to their seats, Mrs. Pepperpot heard someone sniffling and crying in a little room next to the stage.

100

BJÖRN BERG
DID THESE DRAWINGS!
"BJÖRN" MEANS "BEAR"
IN SWEDISH.
IF HE'S BARE,
MAYBE WE
SHOULD SEND HIM
SOME CLOTHES!

"That's funny!" she thought and peeped through the door. There she saw a man with a top hat and long moustache, sitting on a chair, crying like a baby.

"Well, I never!" said Mrs. Pepperpot, but before she had time to follow the rest of her party, she *shrank*!

As she stood there, a tiny figure by the door in her bright summer dress and little straw hat, the puppeteer saw her at once. Quick as a flash he stretched out his hand and picked her up.

"*There* you are!" he said, holding her tightly between finger and thumb. "I thought I'd lost you!"

Mrs. Pepperpot was so terrified she didn't move, but when the man took a closer look, he said, "But you're not my Sleeping Beauty at all!"

"Of course I'm not!" said Mrs. Pepperpot. "The very idea!"

"All the same," said the puppet man, "since I can't find my most important puppet, you'll have to play her part. You'll look fine with a blond wig and a crown and a veil, and I'll make your face up so that you'll be really beautiful."

"You let me go this minute!" shouted Mrs. Pepperpot, struggling to get out of the man's grip. "Whoever heard of an old woman like me playing Sleeping Beauty?"

"Now, now! You have talent—you can act, I'm sure of it. And that's more than can be said of my other puppets who have to be handled with sticks and threads. You can walk and talk by yourself; you're just what I've always dreamed of, and you'll bring me success and lots of money, you'll see."

"Over my dead body!" said Mrs. Pepperpot, who was still furious. "I don't even remember the story of Sleeping Beauty."

"I shall be telling the story," explained the puppet man, "and you just have to do the things I say. But you don't come into the first act at all, so you can stand at the side and watch the other puppets through that crack in the curtain. Now it's time for the show to start, so be a sport and stay there, won't you?"

"I may and I may not," said Mrs. Pepperpot. So he lifted her gingerly down on the side of the puppet stage, which was set up in the middle of the real theater stage.

Then the lights in the studio went out and those on the little stage went on. Mrs. Pepperpot peeped through the hole in the curtain. The scene was a magnificent marble hall, and she could see a puppet king and queen sitting on their thrones with their courtiers standing around. They were looking at a baby doll in a cradle.

The man began to speak behind the stage.

"There was once a king and a queen who had been blessed with a baby princess."

"Lucky he didn't want me to lie in the cradle!" thought Mrs. Pepperpot.

The man read on, telling how the good fairies were asked to the christening party and how they each gave the little princess a gift. Waving their wands over her cradle, the fairies came in one by one.

"May you have the gift of Beauty!" said one.

"May you have the gift of Patience!" said another.

"I could certainly do with that gift," said Mrs. Pepperpot to herself. "If there's anything I lack, it's patience!"

When all the good fairies except one had waved their wands over the cradle, there was a terrible clap of thunder and the stage went completely dark for a moment.

"Goodness gracious!" cried Mrs. Pepperpot. "I hope they haven't had a breakdown!" She was beginning to get excited about the play now.

The lights went on again, and there was the bad fairy leaning over the baby with her wand.

"Ha, ha!" said the puppeteer in an old witch sort of voice. "Today you are all happy, but this is *my* gift to the princess; in your fifteenth year may you prick your finger on a spindle and die!" And with that the bad fairy vanished in another clap of thunder and blackout.

"Well, if I'm the Sleeping Beauty, I'm a good deal more than fifteen years old and I'm still hale and hearty!" thought Mrs. Pepperpot.

The puppeteer now brought on another fairy to tell the king and queen that their daughter would not really die, but only go into a long, long sleep.

"One day a prince will come and wake her up," said the fairy, and that was the end of the first act.

The puppeteer was glad to see Mrs. Pepperpot still standing there, but he didn't take any chances and caught her up roughly before she could protest. No matter how much she wriggled, she was dressed in the princess's blond wig with a crown on top and a veil down her back. The worst part was when the man made up her face. "Ugh! It tastes like candle wax!" she cried.

But when at last he put her down in front of a little mirror, she had to admit she looked rather wonderful.

"Now listen," said the puppeteer, "I don't mind if you make up your own speeches, but you must follow the story as I tell it, and one thing you must remember—no advertising! It's strictly forbidden on this TV station."

"Is it indeed!" said Mrs. Pepperpot, who had not forgiven him for the rough treatment she had had—why, he had even pulled her hair! "We'll see about that!" she muttered.

But there was no time to argue, because the man was preparing to raise the curtain again. The scene was the same as before, but at first there were no puppets on the stage. The puppeteer read the introduction to the next part of the story.

"The king was so anxious to keep his only child safe from all harm, that he ordered every spindle in the country burned and forbade any more to be made. Meanwhile the princess grew up with all the gifts she had received from the fairies; she was good and beautiful, modest and patient, and everyone loved her. Then one day, when she was fifteen years old, the king and queen had gone out and she was all alone in the palace. She thought she would explore a bit."

The man stopped reading and whispered to Mrs. Pepperpot, "This is where you come in! Walk across the marble hall and up the winding staircase in the corner. You'll find the bad fairy at the top, spinning."

He gave her a little push, and Mrs. Pepperpot, in all her princess finery, walked onto the stage as grandly as she could. In the middle of the marble hall she stood still and looked for the staircase. When she saw it, she turned to the audience and, pointing to the stairs, she said, "I have to go up there; I hope it's safe! Always buy planks at Banks, the lumber man!" And up she went, holding her long skirt like a lady.

At the top of the stairs she found the bad fairy puppet sitting, turning her spindle in her hand.

"Why, whatever are you doing with that old-fashioned thing?" asked Mrs. Pepperpot.

"I am spinning," said the puppeteer in his old witch voice.

"I call that silly," said Mrs. Pepperpot, "when you can buy the best knitting wool in town at Lamb's Wool Shop!"

The audience laughed at this, but the man was not amused. However, he couldn't stop now, so he went on with the play, saying in his old witch voice, "Would you like to spin, my child?"

"I don't mind if I do," said Mrs. Pepperpot. As she took the spindle from the bad fairy's hand, the man whispered to her to pretend to prick herself.

"Ouch!" cried Mrs. Pepperpot, sucking her finger and shaking it. "I need a plaster from Mr. Sands, the druggist!"

Again the audience laughed. The man now whispered to her to lie down on the bed and go to sleep. She asked if he wanted her to snore to make it more lifelike.

"Of course not!" he said angrily. "And I don't want any advertising for sleeping pills either!"

"Not necessary!" said Mrs. Pepperpot, making herself comfortable on the bed. Then she raised her head for a moment, and in a singsong voice she spoke to the people in the audience:

> *The moment you recline*
> *On a mattress from Irvine*
> *You will fall into a sleep*
> *That is really quite divine!*

The puppeteer had difficulty making himself heard through the shouts of laughter. But at last he was able to go on with the story of how the princess slept for a hundred years and everyone in the palace slept too. When he got to the part about the rose hedge growing thicker and thicker around the walls of the palace, Mrs. Pepperpot popped her head up again and said:

> *Quick-growing roses*
> *From Ratlin and Moses*

and then pretended to sleep again. She was really getting her revenge on the puppeteer, and she was enjoying every minute of it.

The man struggled on, but now the audience laughed at everything that was said, and he began to wonder if he should stop the show. He tried reading again. "At length the king's son came to the narrow stairs in the tower. When he reached the top, he opened the door of the little chamber, and there he saw the most beautiful sight he had ever seen—the Sleeping Beauty."

From the record player came soft music to suit the scene, as the puppet prince walked up the stairs and came through the door. Mrs. Pepperpot winked at the audience and said:

I owe my beautiful skin
To Complexion-Milk by Flyn.

The puppet prince walked stiffly over to her bed and stiffly bent down and planted a wooden kiss on her cheek. But this was too much for Mrs. Pepperpot. "No, no!" she shrieked, jumping out of bed and knocking the prince flying, so that all his threads broke and he landed in an untidy heap at the bottom of the stairs.

Down the stairs came Mrs. Pepperpot herself, and, jumping over the fallen prince, she rushed across the stage and out through the curtain, while the audience rolled in their seats and clapped and shouted for the princess to come back.

But once safely in the dressing room, Mrs. Pepperpot only just had time to snatch off her wig and veil and crown before she grew to her normal size. She put the little things in her handbag and walked through the door as calmly as you please, only to be met by the poor puppeteer, who was wringing his hands and crying even worse than before the show.

"What's the matter?" asked Mrs. Pepperpot.

"My show's ruined!" he wailed. "They'll never put it on TV again after all that advertising!"

"Advertising?" Mrs. Pepperpot pretended to be surprised. "Wasn't it all part of the play?"

But the man wasn't listening to her. "Oh dear, oh dear! What will become of me? And now I have no Sleeping Beauty at all!"

"You should treat your puppets with more respect," said Mrs. Pepperpot. "They don't like being pushed around and having their hair pulled!"

With that she left him and walked out to the square to get on the bus. Her friends had all been too busy laughing and discussing the play to notice that she hadn't been with them. She sat down next to Sarah South who asked her if she had enjoyed the show.

"Oh, I had a lovely time!—we all did, I mean!" said Mrs. Pepperpot.

Teskedsgumman

108

"TESKEDSGUMMAN" MEANS "TEASPOON-LADY" IN SWEDISH! ITS ANOTHER WAY TO SAY THAT MRS. PEPPERPOT IS VERY TINY

IF YOU DONT SHOWING OF GOING TO YOU!

As I went out a Crow
In a low voice said, "Oh,
I was looking for you.
How do you do?
I just came to tell you
To tell Lesley (will you?)
That her little Bluebird
Wanted me to bring word
That the north wind last night
That made the stars bright
And made ice on the trough
Almost made him cough
His tail feathers off.
He just had to fly!
But he sent her Good-by,
And said to be good,
And wear her red hood,
And look for skunk tracks
In the snow with an ax—
And do everything!
And perhaps in the spring
He would come back and sing."

The Last Word of a Bluebird
as Told to a Child

by Robert Frost

dv Szekeres

What Makes a Bird a Bird?

by May Garelick

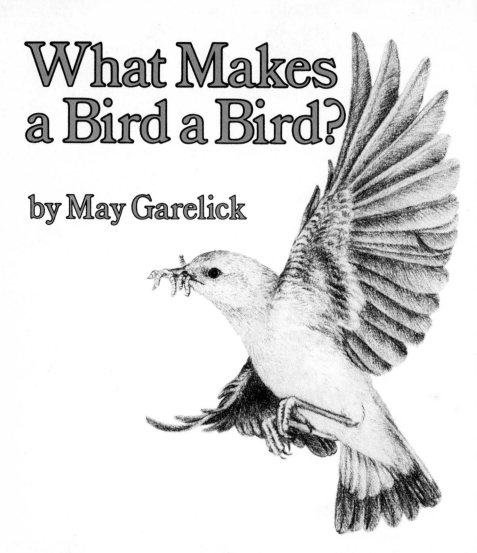

I n trees and in bushes, at the edge of a brook, on the ground, and in the air, birds are flying, singing, calling, bathing, nesting.

How do we know that a bird is a bird? What makes it a bird?

Illustrated by Eva Hülsmann

Is it a bird because it flies?

A fly flies. So do butterflies, ladybugs, dragonflies, and bees. But these are not birds. They are insects.

Many insects fly. Not as fast as birds, not as far as birds, but many insects fly.

And what is this, flying around in the middle of the night?

It's not an insect.

It's not a bird.

It's a bat.

All day bats hang upside down, asleep in hollow trees or in caves. At night they fly, catching insects to eat as they fly around.

Bats fly, insects fly, birds fly, and other things fly, too.

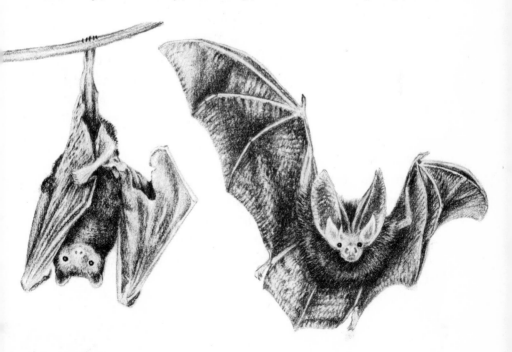

What do you think this is, flying above the water?

Is it a bat? An insect? A bird? No, it's a flying fish that has been frightened by an enemy under water. Like all fish, a flying fish lives most of the time in water. But if an enemy comes near, it can jump up out of the water, dart through the air, and escape.

Flying fish don't fly high and they don't fly far, but they fly higher and farther than some *birds*.

If there are flying insects, flying bats, and even flying fish, then it's not flying that makes a bird a bird.

As a matter of fact, you know a *bird* that doesn't fly.

Have you ever seen a chicken fly? Hardly ever. Sometimes a chicken tries to fly. But it doesn't get far. To get anywhere a chicken walks.

Is a chicken a bird? Yes.

Can you think of another bird that can't fly?

A penguin can't fly. Penguins walk. Down to the water they waddle, and into the sea for a swim.

The penguin's little wings are like flippers. They're fine for swimming, but too small to lift the penguin up into the air.

112

Another bird that doesn't fly is the ostrich.

It's the biggest bird in the world, but it can't fly. An ostrich can run fast, though—even faster than a horse. No wonder. Look at those long legs. That's why the ostrich is such a fast runner.

If the ostrich can't fly, and penguins and chickens can't fly, what makes them birds?

Are they birds because they have wings?

Birds have wings, all right. But look at a fly flying around. You can see its wings. And dragonflies and butterflies and bees have wings, too.

Not all insects have wings, but those that fly have to have wings. Anything that flies has to have wings.

Then what about a chicken and an ostrich? They have wings, but do not fly. Why? Their wings are too small to lift their bodies up in the air.

Still an ostrich, a chicken, and a penguin are birds. So it isn't wings that make a bird a bird.

Is a bird a thing that sings?

Birds sing and call to each other, especially in the spring. Some birds sing, some birds call, some cluck, some quack. That's how birds talk to each other.

One bird's song may mean, "This is my tree. Keep away." Usually other birds do keep away. If they don't, there's a fight.

A mother hen clucks to her chicks to tell them that food is here.

"Cluck, cluck." And her baby chicks come running.

A duck quacks to her ducklings.

"Quack, quack." And her ducklings follow her.

"Peep, peep," call the baby robins. And their parents know that the babies are hungry.

Birds sing and call messages to each other. But singing and calling is not what makes a bird a bird.

Lots of *insects* sing and call their messages to each other, too.

Crickets chirp, and grasshoppers hum. Katydids repeat their rhythmic song all night long. "Katydid, katydid, katy didn't." And of all the insects, the tree cricket's song at night is the most beautiful. But these singers and callers are not birds. So it isn't singing that makes a bird a bird.

Then what *is* the special thing that makes a bird a bird?

Is it a bird if it builds a nest?

Birds build nests in trees, in bushes, under eaves, in barns. Sometimes they even build nests in mailboxes, wherever their eggs and their babies will be safe.

Birds' eggs must be kept warm in order to hatch. The nest and the mother's body keep the eggs warm.

But some birds build no nests at all. A whippoorwill lays her eggs on the ground. But the eggs are the color of the ground around them—camouflaged—so they are safe.

The penguin that lives in the cold, icy Antarctic builds no nest. The mother lays one egg. Then the father penguin carries the egg on top of his feet, close to his body. That's how he keeps the egg warm for two months, until it is ready to hatch.

Other creatures make nests. Ants and bees, snakes and fish, and rabbits and mice make nests.

Nest building is not the special thing that makes a bird a bird.

116

HEY- CRICKET, YOU FLY —
AND YOU HAVE WINGS,
AND YOU SING LIKE ANYTHING,
AND YOU BUILD NESTS, AND
LADY CRICKETS LAY EGGS —
WHY ARENT YOU A BIRD?

'CAUSE I'D
RATHER BE
A CRICKET!

FLEAS HAVE
MORE FUN

Neither is egg-laying. All birds lay eggs, it's true. But so do frogs, snakes, fish, bees, mosquitoes, and many other creatures.

So—it's not flying that makes a bird different from anything else alive.

And it's not having wings.

And it's not singing or calling.

And it's not building nests or laying eggs.

What is it, then, that makes a bird a bird?

Birds have something that no other living thing has. What is it?

FEATHERS!

Only birds have feathers. That's the special thing that makes a bird a bird. A bird has to have feathers to be a bird.

If it flies or not, if it sings or not; anything with feathers is a bird.

Feathers are strong. Try to break or tear one, and you'll see how strong a feather is. Bend a feather so the tip touches the bottom. Watch it spring back. It won't break.

Feathers are light. Hold a feather and you'll see how light it is. You've heard people say that something is "light as a feather."

Feathers are beautiful. They come in all colors. There are red cardinals, blue blue jays, black blackbirds, white doves, green parrots, brown sparrows, and many other birds in other colored feathers.

Feathers are useful, too.

They do many things for birds. Their flight feathers make birds the best flyers. Even though other creatures fly, no living creature can fly as long or as far as a bird.

A bird has several layers of feathers. There's a cloak of feathers that helps keep birds warm in winter. Watch a bird on a cold day. It looks like a fat puffball because it has fluffed out its feathers to keep out the cold.

A layer of flat feathers helps keep birds cool in summer. The heat from the bird's body works its way out through these feathers.

Feathers help keep birds dry in the rain. Put a drop of water on a feather, and watch the water slide off.

Birds take good care of their feathers. Some birds bathe in water—ducking, splashing, spreading their wings. Some birds bathe in fine dust. After bathing, they preen their feathers carefully with their beaks. From an oil sac at the tail, birds take oil into their beaks to soften and straighten their feathers.

But no matter how well birds clean their feathers, they get brittle and wear out. About once a year birds molt—their worn out feathers fall out. Not all at once, just one or two at a time. And as they fall out, new feathers grow in.

You may find some of these old feathers on the ground. Pick them up and look at them.

Feathers are the special things that *make a bird a bird.*

118

Ten Little Crickadees
by Elaine Livermore

Ten little birds are hiding in this picture. Can you find them?

How Did Mary Poppins Find Me?

by P.L. Travers

Where do ideas come from? Have you any idea where you get an idea? So many people—many of them children—have asked me where I got the idea for Mary Poppins. They want to know whether she is taken from somebody in real life, or whether she is just invented. But how could she be taken from somebody in real life? Did *you* ever know anybody who slid *up* the banisters? On the other hand, who could have "just invented" somebody who slides up banisters and flies from place to place with no other means of propulsion than a parrot-headed umbrella?

These are tricky questions, and I never knew how to answer them till Hendrick Willem van Loon, who wrote and drew so many things for children, came hurrying to my rescue. "No one thought her up," he told me. "She's an idea that came looking for *you!*" And as he was speaking, the idea of three dancing elephants apparently came looking for him, for he drew them for me on the back of an envelope.

But why me? I wanted to know. Why didn't she happen to somebody else? And then I remembered that a boy of sixteen had once asked me to promise him never to become clever. Well, it was a strange request but one I could readily agree to—though of course I wanted to know what he meant. "I've just been reading *Mary Poppins* again," he told me, "and it could only have been written by a special sort of lunatic!"

120

Well, in a way I understood. To think things up you have to be clever. But to sit still and let them happen to you clearly needs something else. Maybe a kind of listening. Perhaps Lewis Carroll sat still and listened and the idea of Alice in Wonderland came by and tapped him on the shoulder. Perhaps the world is full of ideas, all of them looking for the right person. If so, all you have to do—in addition to being a lunatic—is simply to sit quite still and listen and one of them may happen to you.

Mary Poppins books by Pamela Travers are:
Mary Poppins
Mary Poppins Comes Back
Mary Poppins Opens the Door
Mary Poppins in the Park
Mary Poppins from A to Z
all illustrated by Mary Shepard

LAKES

by Ann Nolan Clark
Drawing by Bob Totten

Lakes
Are the holding places
For water,
As the fireplace
Is the holding place
For fire,
As the plaza
Is the holding place
For people.
I know a lake in the mountains.
My Grandfather told me about it.
My Father told me.
My Mother's Brother told me.
But my heart is the holding place,
My heart is the keeping place
For the things I know
About the lake in the mountains.

Always will I keep
In my heart
The things that belong there,
As lakes
Keep water
For the people.

JOKER

by *Elizabeth Coatsworth*

This is the story of Joker;
It's like an old, old song;
His heart was great
In love and hate,
And his memory was long.

oker was born on the Circle M ranch in Montana. As a colt he ran with his mother and the other ranch horses in the great pastures at the foot of the mountains. He played with the colts born in his year and learned wisdom from his wise old mother. In the mornings he heard the song of the larks, and at dusk the coyotes' howl was his lullaby.

From the beginning Joker was unusually small, round-bodied, and strong. But the remarkable thing about him was his color. Probably there was no other horse in the world quite like him.

On one side he appeared to be a pure white pony with a black tail and a little black cap on the top of his head. But on the other side he seemed all black, with white socks, a white mane, and a milk-white nose. Like his mother, he was a pinto, but instead of being spotted like other pintos, his color was divided in two at the spine.

JOE KRUSH

DID THESE ILLUSTRATIONS!
HE'S A JOKER, TOO!
ME SAVVY,
KEMO SABE!

Mr. Al, the owner of the ranch, didn't notice Joker until the second summer, when he rode out with a buyer to look over the young stock.

"That's a nice looking white foal over there," the buyer said. Tex, one of the cowboys, cut Joker out from the other horses to join the colts that were going off in the four big trucks. But when the buyer came to look for his white colt, he was nowhere to be found.

"Tex, where's that white colt?" Mr. Al shouted.

Tex grinned and flapped his hat at a black colt that was trying to jump the corral gate. The colt whirled, and there he was! No longer a black colt with a white mane, but a snow-white colt with black trimmings.

"There's a joker," Mr. Al said to the buyer. "You're getting two horses for the price of one."

But to himself he thought, "If I had a boy now, I'd save that pony for him."

Mr. Al didn't have a boy, and Mrs. Al said they'd better not go looking for one or they'd make a mistake. In good time a boy would come to them, she said.

"How'll we know he's the right one?" Mr. Al would ask.

"Oh, we'll know," said Mrs. Al. But no boy had come yet.

While the truck with Joker in it moved down the highway by the pasture, Joker's mother followed along the fence, whinnying and whinnying sharp and loud, and from the truck Joker whinnied back to her. She was an old mare and that spring she had no colt, so perhaps she loved Joker doubly.

All day and all night the trucks travelled through strange country, and at last they came to the place where the buyer lived at the edge of a city. And there, in the weeks that followed, the young horses were broken in to harness. The buyer was a patient man and he liked horses. Joker and the others were not badly treated. When Joker's education was finished, he was a perfect saddle pony, gentle, intelligent, and strong, with good gaits and a good mouth. If he still remembered pastures—far away where the wild duck rose from the river and an old mare whinnied for her colt—there was no way that anyone would know.

One day in the spring, when Joker was two years old, the buyer sold him to Mr. Selwyn, a wealthy man who lived near the country club. Mr. Selwyn wanted to give the pony to his son Ross for a birthday present, and he had paid extra for Joker because of his peculiar coloring.

Ross Selwyn was a show-off, and he didn't know or care much about horses, or how they felt. He was delighted with Joker and soon saw how gentle and willing he was.

But Ross wanted to be admired, and he loved to play tricks on people. As he rode Joker past friends, he would suddenly spin him around, with a dig of a spur and a jerk of the curb and a cut of the quirt. Everyone, suddenly seeing a black pony turn white, or a white pony turn black, would laugh and applaud, and Ross would spin Joker around full circle and ride on, all smiles.

But Joker soon dreaded the boy's hand on the rein, and his foot in the stirrup.

One day the good-natured, well-trained pony ran away and scraped Ross out of the saddle. Someone caught Joker, and when Ross got him home, he took the carriage whip and beat him.

The stableman tried to interfere. "You'll only teach him to kick. He's a good pony if he's rightly treated."

But Ross knew better.

"I'll teach you," he kept saying over and over through his teeth, and he did teach Joker. He taught him to rear and buck and bite and strike out with his front feet and lash out with his hind feet. He taught him to fight his rider with all his wit and courage. Very soon, of course, Ross didn't dare ride him at all, but used him to play jokes of another kind. When boys came to spend the day with him, Ross would offer to let them ride his pinto, and so round and pretty did Joker look, and so quietly did he stand while he was being saddled, that at first the boys were eager to ride him.

But some he threw at once by bucking, and some later by running under the young oak tree by the drive, and some by shying at the mailbox near the gate, and some by rearing in the road. And then how Ross would laugh!

"I told you his name was Joker," he would say. "Be a sport! The joke's on you."

Soon very few boys came to play with Ross, and no boys at all would ride Ross's pinto pony. For days Joker stood in the paddock, as plump and pretty as a two-colored partridge, but with only one desire in his heart: To be home again, to be running with the horses of the Circle M ranch while the mountains climbed the sky and the Herefords bawled under the cottonwoods in the wash.

One day there appeared at the stable a boy of about fifteen, looking for work. He told the stableman and the gardener that his name was Bill, and that he was an orphan raised in the cattle country. His father had died about a month earlier and the bank had taken their place. Bill had a dollar and seventeen cents in the pocket of his blue jeans and it was all he had in the world, though he didn't tell the men that. Nor did he tell them that he'd been looking for work in the city for a week and hadn't found any.

While Bill was talking to the stableman, Ross slid in as quietly as a hunting cat and listened.

"Dad'll be home for lunch," he told Bill. "You'd better wait. Say, would you like to ride my pony while you wait?"

Bill shook his head.

"Guess not," he said, leaning against the paddock fence, hands in his jeans pockets. He didn't feel like riding someone else's pony. The bank had taken his.

"Give you a dollar."

Bill needed a dollar but he didn't like Ross. He shook his head.

Ross was accustomed to having his own way.

"If you ride the pony, you can have him," he said.

He was sure no one could ride Joker, and he wanted to see this new boy thrown. It would serve him right for not being polite enough to do what he was asked to do.

Bill gave Ross a long look. Then he looked at Joker.

"Throws everyone," the stableman said under his breath. Bill heard him.

"All right. I'll ride him," he said.

Ross was delighted.

As usual, Joker stood perfectly quiet while his bridle was put on and the saddle girths tightened. Bill swung into the saddle.

Ross began to grin.

But Joker felt something he had not felt for a long time. Someone was sitting on his back who had good balance and a light hand on the rein. A quiet voice spoke to him. He moved forward.

"Hi yah," shouted Ross, waving his hat, anxious for the fun to begin.

But Joker didn't buck.

He didn't sidle under the low branches of the young oak.

He didn't shy at the mailbox or rear as he reached the road.

Instead, he turned north and broke into an easy lope.

"Here! Come back here!" shouted Ross.

Already Bill was trying to turn Joker's head, but the pony had the bit in his teeth. He was not running away. He was going at an effortless pace, one that he could keep up mile after mile.

"You seem to know where you're going," Bill said to him. "It's more than I can say. Perhaps I'd better just go along with you."

"Stop, thief!" screamed Ross far behind them.

"You said he could have the horse," said the stableman.

"I heard you myself," said the gardener.

"But I never thought he could stay on him," whined Ross.

"Oh, but that pony's a joker!" said the stableman.

"Yes, he sure is a joker!" said the gardener.

On the road leading to the mountains a boy on a two colored horse was riding toward Circle M ranch, where the eagles swung far up into the sky and Mr. and Mrs. Al waited for the son who someday would come to them, as naturally as an apple grows on an apple tree. The ranch was far, far away, but a horse will always find the place where he was foaled. Joker had no doubts. He was travelling easily with a light heart, and for the first time since his father's death, Bill's heart too was light, though he scarcely knew why.

He had a horse and a dollar and seventeen cents, and now, in the distance, he could see the mountains. Everything would be all right.

This is the story of Joker,
And it ends like a happy song;
His heart was great
In love and hate,
And his memory was long.

DIME ILLUSION

Can you place a dime flat on this picture of a table in such a way that the dime does not touch any of the four sides of the table top?

It certainly looks possible, but when you try it, you will discover that the dime is too large. The illusion is caused partly by the angle of perspective in the drawing and partly by the fact that dimes are a bit larger than we remember them to be.

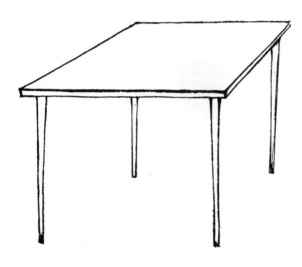

by Martin Gardner

THE TELEPHONE

Adapted from the Russian by William Jay Smith
(in collaboration with Max Hayward)

The telephone rang.
"Hello! Who's there?"
"The Polar Bear."
"What do you want?"
"I'm calling for the Elephant."
"What does *he* want?"
"He wants a little
Peanut brittle."
"Peanut brittle! . . . And for whom?"
"It's for his little
Elephant sons."
"How much does he want?"
"Oh, five or six tons.
Right now that's all
That they can manage—they're quite small."

Illustrated by Blair Lent

The telephone rang. The Crocodile
Said, with a tear:
"My dearest dear,
We don't need umbrellas or mackintoshes;
My wife and baby need new galoshes;
Send us some, please!"
"Wait—wasn't it you
Who just last week ordered two
Pairs of beautiful brand-new galoshes?"
"Oh, those that came last week—they
Got gobbled up right away;
And we just can't wait
For supper tonight—
We'd like to sprinkle on our goulashes
One or two dozen delicious galoshes!"
The telephone rang. The Turtle Doves
Said: "Send us, please, some long white gloves!"
It rang again; the Chimpanzees
Giggled: "Phone books, please!"
The telephone rang. The Grizzly Bear
Said: "Grr! Grr!"

"Stop, Bear. Don't growl; don't bawl!
Just tell me what you want!"
But on he went: "Grr! Grrrrrrr!"
Why? What for?
I couldn't make out;
I just banged down the receiver.
The telephone rang. The Flamingos
Said: "Rush us over a bottle of those
Little pink pills!
We've swallowed every frog in the lake,
And are croaking with a stomach ache!"
The Pig telephoned. Ivan Pigtail
Said: "Send over Nina Nightingale!
Together, I bet,
We'll sing a duet
That opera lovers will never forget!
I'll begin—"
"No, you won't! The divine Nightingale
Accompany a Pig! Ivan Petrovich,

No!
You'd better call on Katya Crow!"
The telephone rang. The Polar Bear
Said: "Come to the aid of the Walrus, sir!
He's about
      to choke
           on a fat
               oyster!"
And so it goes. The whole day long
The same silly song:
      Ting-a-ling!
          Ting-a-ling!
             Ting-a-ling!
I haven't slept for three whole nights.
I'm dead.
I'd really like to go to bed
And get some sleep.
But every time I lay down my head
The telephone rings.

"Who's there? Hello!"
"It's the Rhino."
"What's wrong, Rhino?"
"Terrible trouble.
Come on the double!"
"What's the matter? Why the fuss?"
"Quick. Save him—"
"Who?"
"The Hippopotamus.
He's sinking out there in that awful swamp. . . ."
"In the swamp?"
"Yes, he's stuck.
And if you don't come right away,
He'll drown in that terrible damp
And dismal swamp.
He'll die; he'll croak—oh, oh, oh,
Poor Hippo-
       po-
         po . . . ."
"Okay. I'm coming
Right away!"
Whew! What a job! You need a truck
To help a Hippo when he's stuck!

Table of Tens

S. Carl Hirsch

One morning long ago, Thomas Jefferson climbed into his horse-drawn buggy and left his fine house in Virginia. He was traveling to the nation's capital, Washington, D.C., where he had served as President of the United States.

The summer morning was quiet, except for the clip-clop of the horse trotting along the country road. But Jefferson frowned. From the sound of the hoofbeats, he could tell something was wrong. His horse was limping slightly.

"Easy, Molly," he called out to the little mare in a soothing voice. "We'll get you a new shoe in the next town."

As the horse moved along, Jefferson could hear the tinkle of a bell that he had attached to the back of the buggy together with a wheel for measuring distance. This wheel was much smaller than the two wheels of the buggy, and every time it turned one hundred times, the bell rang. After ten rings of the bell, the traveler knew that he had covered exactly one mile.

Jefferson was not only a great patriot, but also a scientist and inventor who liked to make things with his hands. But his greatest wish was to solve the many puzzling problems that faced the young United States.

Margot Tomes DREW THESE ILLUSTRATIONS

THEY'RE SPLENDID!

137

For example, there was the troublesome matter of America's coins. The new nation was made up of people from many lands. They had brought with them their many kinds of money. And these were the coins with which people bought and sold goods, received their wages, and paid their debts.

What confusion for the poor storekeeper! He tried to read the words on French, Spanish, and Dutch coins but had little idea about their value. In addition, each of the colonies of America had its own kind of coins, adding to the muddle of America's money.

For this problem, Jefferson gave the nation a simple solution. He held up his hands, explaining to the Congress of the United States that since ancient times men had counted on their fingers. That is why, he pointed out, the world uses a system of counting based on the number ten. In planning a new system of coins, suggested Jefferson, America would be wise to use the simple table of tens.

The counting system has ten numbers, and as a schoolboy in Virginia, Jefferson had learned the table of tens. "Count to ten; then start over again," the schoolmaster taught his pupils.

"Most of us are schoolboys throughout life," Jefferson declared, "and we need coins which any child can understand."

Jefferson's plan began with the penny. Ten pennies were a dime. And ten dimes were equal to a dollar. What could be easier than that? All of America agreed, and the United States became the first country in the world to have coins based on the table of tens.

Still another problem for America was its weights and measures. Few people knew the exact area of an acre of land. A bushel of apples was one size in North Carolina and another size in New Hampshire.

Silversmiths and grocers worked with unlike systems of weights. Printers and carpenters used different terms of measurement in their work. To this day, America still uses a jumble of odd terms, such as pennyweights and grains, rods and yards, pecks and pints, which have no clear relationship with each other.

Jefferson offered a new plan. But he could not get Congress to adopt it. As he grew old, he returned many times

to the capital to plead for a simple system of weights and measures. But the congressmen would not listen to him.

On this summer morning the aged Jefferson was journeying once more to Washington, D. C. In a tiny village along his route, he found a blacksmith who made a new shoe for his limping horse.

"How far did you ride today, sir?" asked the blacksmith.

"I'll answer that question for you in a strange way," Jefferson replied with a twinkle in his eyes, and as the blacksmith watched with much curiosity, Jefferson checked the mileage shown on his little third wheel.

"Now, let us say a mile is like a dollar," explained the statesman. "In that case, I have traveled nine dollars, two dimes, and three cents."

The blacksmith was puzzled for a moment. But soon his face lit up. "Yes, I understand you very well," he said, chuckling.

Jefferson's idea was that not only money but also distances could be measured by the table of tens. The same simple method could be used for measuring the size of a field, the contents of a box, the weight of a bale of cotton, and the speed of a horse and buggy as well.

In almost every country in the world, people are now weighing and measuring by the table of tens. The system they use is called the metric system.

The United States may also change soon to this simple system. Thomas Jefferson had faith that the day would come when Americans would measure by the table of tens. But he did not realize it would take two hundred years!

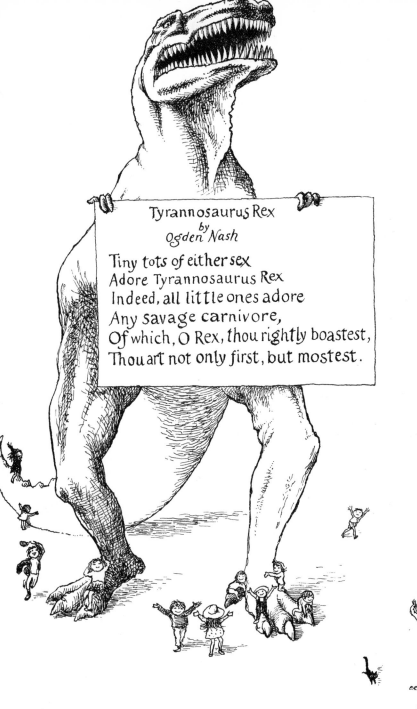

Tyrannosaurus Rex
by
Ogden Nash

Tiny tots of either sex
Adore Tyrannosaurus Rex
Indeed, all little ones adore
Any savage carnivore,
Of which, O Rex, thou rightly boastest,
Thou art not only first, but mostest.

ERIK BLEGVAD

The Song of the Jellicles

Jellicle Cats come out to-night,
Jellicle Cats come one come all:
The Jellicle Moon is shining bright—
Jellicles come to the Jellicle Ball.

Jellicle Cats are black and white,
Jellicle Cats are rather small;
Jellicle Cats are merry and bright,
And pleasant to hear when they caterwaul.
Jellicle Cats have cheerful faces,
Jellicle Cats have bright black eyes;
They like to practice their airs and graces
And wait for the Jellicle Moon to rise.

Jellicle Cats develop slowly,
Jellicle Cats are not too big;
Jellicle Cats are roly-poly,
They know how to dance a gavotte and a jig.
Until the Jellicle Moon appears
They make their toilette and take their repose:
Jellicles wash behind their ears,
Jellicles dry between their toes.

Jellicle Cats are white and black,
Jellicle Cats are of moderate size;
Jellicles jump like a jumping-jack,
Jellicle Cats have moonlit eyes.
They're quiet enough in the morning hours,
They're quiet enough in the afternoon,
Reserving their terpsichorean powers
To dance by the light of the Jellicle Moon.

142

"TERPSICHOREAN"
MEANS DANCING

by T.S. Eliot

Jellicle Cats are black and white,
Jellicle Cats (as I said) are small;
If it happens to be a stormy night
They will practice a caper or two in the hall.
If it happens the sun is shining bright
You would say they had nothing to do at all:
They are resting and saving themselves to be
    right
For the Jellicle Moon and the Jellicle Ball.

who are you, little i

(five or six years old)
peering from some high

window; at the gold

of november sunset

(and feeling: that if day
has to become night

this is a beautiful way)

by e. e. cummings

the Fools of Chelm
and the Stupid Carp

by Isaac Bashevis Singer

T his took place in Chelm, a city of fools. Where else could it have happened? Every housewife in Chelm bought fish for the Sabbath. The rich bought large fish, the poor small ones. They were bought on Thursday, cut up, chopped, and made into gefilte fish on Friday, and eaten on the Sabbath.

One Thursday morning the door opened at the house of the community leader of Chelm, Gronam the Ox, and Feivel Ninny entered, carrying a trough full of water. Inside was a large, live carp.

"What is this?" Gronam asked.

"A gift to you from the wise men of Chelm," Feivel said. "It is the largest carp ever caught in the Lake of Chelm, and we all decided to give it to you as a token of appreciation for your great wisdom."

145

Illustrated by David McPhail

"Thank you very much," Gronam the Ox replied. "My wife, Yenta Pesha, will be delighted. She and I both love carp. I read in a book that eating the brains of a carp increases wisdom, and even though we in Chelm are immensely clever, a little improvement never hurts. But let me have a close look at him. I was told that a carp's tail shows the size of his brain."

Gronam the Ox was known to be near-sighted, and when he bent down to the trough to better observe the carp's tail, the carp did something that proved he was not as wise as Gronam thought. He lifted his tail and smacked Gronam across the face.

Gronam the Ox was flabbergasted. "Something like this never happened to me before," he exclaimed. "I cannot believe this carp was caught in the Chelm lake. A Chelm carp would know better."

"He's the meanest fish I ever saw in my life," agreed Feivel Ninny.

Even though Chelm is a big city, news traveled quickly there. In no time at all the other wise men of Chelm arrived at the house of their leader, Gronam the Ox. Treitel Fool came, and Sendor Donkey, Shmendrick Numskull, Chazkel Pinhead, and Dopey Lekisch. Gronam the Ox was saying, "I'm not going to eat this fish on the Sabbath. This carp is a fool, and malicious to boot. If I eat him, I could become foolish instead of cleverer."

"Then what shall I do with him?" asked Feivel Ninny.

Gronam the Ox put a finger to his head as a sign that he was thinking hard. After a while he cried out, "No man or animal in Chelm should slap Gronam the Ox. This fish should be punished."

"What kind of punishment shall we give him?" asked

146

Treitel Fool. "All fish are killed anyhow, and one cannot kill a fish twice."

"He shouldn't be killed like other fish," Sendor Donkey said. "He should die in a different way to show that no one can smack our beloved sage, Gronam the Ox, and get away with it."

"What kind of death?" wondered Shmendrick Numskull. "Shall we perhaps just imprison him?"

"There is no prison in Chelm for fish," said Chazkel Pinhead. "And to build such a prison would take too long."

"Maybe he should be hanged," suggested Dopey Lekisch.

"How do you hang a carp?" Feivel Ninny wanted to know. "A creature can be hanged only by its neck, but since a carp has no neck, how will you hang him?"

"My advice is that he should be thrown to the dogs alive," said Treitel Fool.

"It's no good," Gronam the Ox answered. "Our Chelm dogs are both smart and modest, but if they eat this carp, they may become as stupid and mean as he is."

"So what should we do?" all the wise men asked.

"This case needs lengthy consideration," Gronam the Ox decided. "Let's leave the carp in the trough and ponder the matter as long as is necessary. Being the wisest man in Chelm, I cannot afford to pass a sentence that will not be admired by all the Chelmites."

"If the carp stays in the trough a long time, he may die," Feivel Ninny, a former fish dealer, explained. "To keep him alive we must put him into a large tub, and the water has to be changed often. He must also be fed properly."

"You are right, Feivel," Gronam the Ox told him. "Go and find the largest tub in Chelm and see to it that the carp

FOR YOU CRICKETS WHO DON'T KNOW ABOUT JEWISH FOOD — CHALLAH IS A KIND OF DELICIOUS EGG BREAD, MADE IN A LONG, BRAIDED LOAF. GEFILTE FISH IS LITTLE FISH CAKES MADE WITH FINELY GROUND WHITE FISH (LIKE CARP)

148

is kept alive and healthy until the day of judgement. When I reach a decision, you will hear about it."

Of course Gronam's words were the law in Chelm. The five wise men went and found a large tub, filled it with fresh water, and put the criminal carp in it, together with some crumbs of bread, challah, and other tidbits a carp might like to eat. Schlemiel, Gronam's bodyguard, was stationed at the tub to make sure that no greedy Chelmite wife would use the imprisoned carp for gefilte fish.

It just so happened that Gronam the Ox had many other decisions to make, and he kept postponing the sentence. The carp seemed not to be impatient. He ate, swam in the tub, became even fatter than he had been, not realizing that a severe sentence hung over his head. Schlemiel changed the water frequently because he was told that if the carp died, this would be an act of contempt for Gronam the Ox and for the Chelm Court of Justice. Yukel, the water carrier, made a

few extra pennies every day by bringing water for the carp. Some of the Chelmites who were in opposition to Gronam the Ox spread the gossip that Gronam just couldn't find the right type of punishment for the carp, and that he was waiting for the carp to die a natural death. But, as always, a great disappointment awaited them. One morning about a half a year later the sentence became known, and when it was known, Chelm was stunned. The carp had to be drowned.

Gronam the Ox had thought up many clever sentences before, but never one as brilliant as this one. Even his enemies were amazed by this shrewd verdict. Drowning is just the kind of death suited to a spiteful carp with a large tail and a small brain.

That day the entire Chelm community gathered at the lake to see the sentence executed. The carp, which had become almost twice as big as he had been before, was brought to the lake in the wagon that carried the worst criminals to their death. The drummers drummed. Trumpets blared. The Chelmite executioner raised the heavy carp and threw it into the lake with a mighty splash.

A great cry rose from the Chelmites. "Down with the treacherous carp! Long live Gronam the Ox! Hurrah!"

Gronam was lifted by his admirers and carried home with songs of praise. Some Chelmite girls showered him with flowers. Even Yenta Pesha, his wife, who was often critical of Gronam and dared to call him fool, seemed impressed by Gronam's high intelligence.

In Chelm, like everywhere else, there were envious people who found fault with everyone, and they began to say that there was no proof whatsoever that the carp really drowned. Why should a carp drown in lake water? they asked. While hundreds of innocent fish were killed every Friday, they said, that stupid carp lived in comfort for months on the taxpayers' money and then was returned sound and healthy to the lake where he is laughing at Chelm justice.

But only a few listened to these malicious words. They pointed out that months passed and the carp was never caught again, a sure sign that he was dead. It is true that the carp might have just decided to be careful and to avoid the fisherman's net. But how can a foolish carp who slaps Gronam the Ox have such wisdom?

Just the same, to be on the safe side, the wise men of Chelm published a decree that if the nasty carp had refused to be drowned and were caught again, a special jail should be built for him, a pool where he would be kept prisoner for the rest of his life.

The decree was printed in capital letters in the official gazette of Chelm and signed by Gronam the Ox and his five sages—Treitel Fool, Sendor Donkey, Shmendrick Numskull, Chazkel Pinhead, and Dopey Lekisch.

Translated from the Yiddish
by the author and Ruth Schachner Finkel

Meet Your Author

Isaac B. Singer—About Myself

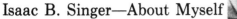

I was born in the village of Raolzymin, Poland, in 1904. When I was three years old, my parents moved to Warsaw, the capital of Poland.

My father was an orthodox rabbi, and our house was a house of holy books and learning. Other children had toys; I played with the books in my father's library. I began to "write" before I even knew the alphabet. I took my father's pen, dipped it in ink, and started to scribble. At school I amazed my fellow students with fantastic stories. Once I told them that my father was a king, and they believed me.

I came to the United States in 1935 and learned to speak English. But I write all of my books first in Yiddish, and then I translate them into English. I have written eleven books for grown-ups and ten for children. I like to write for children. I think they are the best readers. All of my works have been translated into a number of languages.

I live in New York with my wife, Alma. Our son, whose name is Israel, lives in the land of Israel. He is a teacher and a journalist. I have three grandchildren, one girl and two boys.

My hobby is taking long walks in New York. I love birds and all animals, and I believe that men can learn a lot from God's creatures.

153

154

Illustrations by Lee Hill

THE GREAT MINU

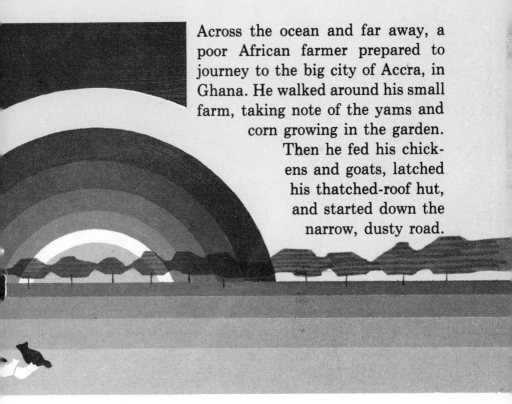

Across the ocean and far away, a poor African farmer prepared to journey to the big city of Accra, in Ghana. He walked around his small farm, taking note of the yams and corn growing in the garden. Then he fed his chickens and goats, latched his thatched-roof hut, and started down the narrow, dusty road.

retold by
BETH P. WILSON

All morning and all afternoon the farmer trudged down the road, stopping only at midday for a bite to eat and a short rest. At last he reached the farms on the outskirts of the city. There he noticed a great herd of cows. Who could own such a great herd, he wondered.
Seeing a man with them, he

156

asked, "To whom do these cows belong?" The man did not know the language of the farmer, who had traveled so far, so he shrugged his shoulders and said, "Minu," meaning "I do not understand." The traveler thought Minu must be a person and exclaimed, "Mr. Minu must be very rich!"

Entering the city, the traveler saw some large new buildings in the town square. He wondered who might own these buildings. But the man he asked could not understand his question, so he also answered, "Minu." "Good heavens!" cried the traveler. "What a rich fellow Mr. Minu must be to own all those cows and these large new buildings, too!"

Soon he came to a grand hotel surrounded by beautiful

grounds and mahogany trees. A group of fashionably-dressed African ladies came down the front steps of the hotel. The traveler stepped up to them and asked who might be the owner of such a grand hotel. The ladies smiled and said softly, "Minu." "How wealthy Mr. Minu is!" exclaimed the astonished traveler.

He wandered from one neighborhood to another and finally came to the harbor where he saw men loading bananas, cocoa beans, and mahogany onto a fine big ship. With the blue sky above, the foamy green ocean below, and the sailors rushing about on board ship, it was an impressive sight. The traveler inquired of a bystander, "To whom does this fine big ship belong?" "Minu," replied the puzzled man who couldn't understand a word of the question. The traveler gasped. "To the great Minu also? He is the richest man I ever heard of!"

Just as the traveler was setting out for home, he saw men carrying a coffin down the main street of Accra. A long procession of people, all dressed in black, followed the men. People on the sidelines shook their heads slowly. Sad faces looked up now and then. When the traveler asked one of the mourners the name of the dead person, he received the usual reply, "Minu."

"Mr. Minu is dead?" wailed the traveler. "Poor Mr. Minu! So he had to leave all his wealth—his great herd of cows, his large new buildings and grand hotel, and his fine big ship—and die just like a poor person. Well, well, in the future I'll be content with my little hut, on my little farm, in my little village."

The long, dusty road back didn't seem as long as it had before. When the farmer arrived home, he unlatched the door of his hut and looked around inside. Then he climbed into his own snug bed and dreamed of the good foo-foo he would eat the next day.

nce upon a time there was a little girl called Little Yellow Riding Hood."

"No! *Red* Riding Hood!"

"Oh yes, of course, Red Riding Hood. Well, one day her mother called and said: 'Little Green Riding Hood—'"

"*Red!*"

"Sorry! Red. 'Now, my child, go to Aunt Mary and take her these potatoes.'"

"No! It doesn't go like that! 'Go to Grandma and take her these cakes.'"

by Gianni Rodari

"All right. So the little girl went off and in the wood she met a giraffe."

"What a mess you're making of it! It was a wolf!"

"And the wolf said: 'What's six times eight?' "
"No! No! The wolf asked her where she was going."

"So he did. And Little Black Riding Hood replied—"

"Red! Red!! Red!!!"

"She replied: 'I'm going to the market to buy some tomatoes.' "
"No, she didn't. She said: 'I'm going to my grandma who is sick, but I've lost my way.' "

"Of course! And the horse said—"
"What horse? It was a wolf."

"So it was. And this is what it said: 'Take the 75 bus, get out at the main square, turn right, and at the first doorway you'll find three steps. Leave the steps where they are, but pick up the dime you'll find lying on them, and buy yourself a packet of chewing gum.'"

"Grandpa, you're terribly bad at telling stories. You get them all wrong. But all the same, I wouldn't mind some chewing gum."

"All right. Here's your dime." And the old man turned back to his newspaper.

Anybody Home?
by Aileen Fisher

I'd like to look
in a meadowy nook
at the small grass house
of a mother mouse
in a velvety blouse.
I'd like to peek
in the door and see
six pink babies
who couldn't see me.

I'd like to spy
in a tree nearby,
on an afternoon
in July or June,
a house in a hole
more deep than high,
and peek inside
at a curled-up 'coon
who sleeps by the sun
and prowls by the moon.

162

Drawings by Eva Hülsmann

I'd like to find
as I rove and roam
a house in a pond
with a mud-packed dome,
and a beaver at home.
I'd like to see
how he looks in there
with a claw for a comb
and his tail for a chair.

I'd like to see
near the top of a tree
a house made of leaves
with rounded eaves
where a squirrel might be
asleep in his clothes
with his tail for a blanket
across his nose.

I'd like to look
in a secret burrow
beside a brook
or a log or furrow,
or under the rocks,
at the house of a fox . . .

or maybe a woodchuck
who likes to whistle . . .

or maybe a badger
with fur a-bristle.

But I'd not look twice,
not even for fun,
if I saw on a bunk
what looked like a *skunk*.
I'd run!

NUTS NATALIE BABBITT

One day the Devil was sitting in his throne room eating walnuts from a large bag and complaining, as usual, about the terrible nuisance of having to crack the shells, when all at once he had an idea. "The best way to eat walnuts," he said to himself, "is to trick someone else into cracking them for you."

So he fetched a pearl from his treasure room, opened the next nut very carefully with a sharp knife so as not to spoil the shell, and put the pearl inside along with the meat. Then he glued the shell back together. "Now all I have to do," he said, "is give this walnut to some greedy soul who'll find the pearl in it and then insist on opening the lot to look for more!"

So he dressed himself as an old man with a long beard and went up into the World, taking along his nutcracker and the bag of walnuts with the special nut on top. And he sat himself down by a country road to wait.

NATALIE BABBITT DREW THE PICTURES TOO!

Pretty soon a farmwife came marching along.

"Hey there!" said the Devil. "Want a walnut?"

The farmwife looked at him shrewdly and was at once suspicious, but she didn't let on for a minute. "All right," she said. "Why not?"

"That's the way," said the Devil, chuckling to himself. And he reached into the bag and took out the special walnut and gave it to her.

However, much to his surprise, she merely cracked the nut open, picked out the meat and ate it, and threw away the shell without a single word. And then she went on her way and disappeared.

"That's strange," said the Devil with a frown. "Either she swallowed my pearl or I gave her the wrong walnut to begin with."

He opened his bag, took out three more nuts that were lying on top of the pile, and cracked them open, but there was no pearl to be seen. He opened four more. Still no pearl. And so it went, on and on all afternoon, till the Devil had opened every walnut in the bag, all by himself after all, and he made a terrible mess on the road with the shells. But he never did find the pearl, and in the end he said to himself, "Well, that's that. She swallowed it."

And there was nothing for it but to go back down to Hell. But he took along a stomachache from eating all those nuts, and a crabby mood that lasted for a week.

In the meantime the farmwife went on to market, where she took the pearl from under her tongue and traded it for two turnips and a butter churn and went back home again well pleased.

We are not all of us greedy.

167

THE DIVER

by Alexander Resnikoff

This time I'll do it! Mommy, look!
I promise I won't be a fool—
I'm going to climb on that diving board
And dive right into the pool!

Look at me, Mom; I'm doing it!
I never have done it before—
I'm climbing those steps to the diving board.
I'll count them: One, two, three, four. . . .

Look, Mom! I'm on the diving board!
This carpet feels terribly rough—
It hurts the tan on the soles of my feet,
But I can take it; I'm tough.

And now I'm jumping up and down
Right by the steps—Mommy, look!
You sure you're looking? Saw me jump?
Now *please*, Mommy, put down that book!

Tiny Drawings by Karen Gundersheimer

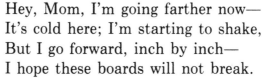

Hey, Mom, I'm going farther now—
It's cold here; I'm starting to shake,
But I go forward, inch by inch—
I hope these boards will not break.

Look at me, Mom! I'm at the end!
I must be a thousand feet high!
Or maybe higher—I'm not sure
I'm looking with only one eye.

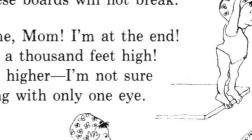

I'll say a prayer, I'll take a deep breath,
I'll hold my nose, and I'll plop—
Maybe you should move a little way back—
Those waves might go over the top!

Mom, are you looking? Watch me now!
I hope that you are prepared—
Look at me, Mommy, here I come—
One. . .
Two. . .
Three. . .
. . . .
. . . .
I am scared. . . .

Oh My darling Sugar Cookie

by Pauline Watson

You will need: 1 bowl, 1 large spoon, 1 measuring c[up?], measuring spoons, and a baking sh[eet?]

Ingredients:

1 cup brown sugar
1 cup soft butter
3 cups flour
1 1/2 teaspoons baking powder
1/2 teaspoon salt
1 egg, slightly beaten
3 tablespoons milk
1 teaspoon vanilla
1/4 cup sugar (to sprinkle over unbaked cookies)

Preheat oven to 400°

Mix in a Bowl to the Tune of CLEMENTINE:

Mash the butter with the sugar,
Stir it twenty times and then,
Add the flour—baking powder,
Add the salt, and stir again.

Add the egg and then the milk, and
Add vanilla, if you please,
Stir and scrunch well with your fingers
Till you work the dough with ease.

Oh my darling, Oh my darling,
Sugar cookies—you are fun!
You will soon be in the oven,
In my tummy when you're done.

Wash your hands and with a teaspoon
Round the dough on baking sheet,
Flatten each round with damp fingers,
Top with sugar for a treat.

Bake 5 to 8 minutes.

Darling Pussycats by Marylin Hafner

In the Middle of the Night
Philippa Pearce

In the middle of the night a fly woke Charlie. At first he lay listening, half-asleep, while it swooped about the room. Sometimes it was far; sometimes it was near—that was what had woken him; and occasionally it was very near indeed. It was very, very near when the buzzing stopped; the fly had alighted on his face. He jerked his head up; the fly buzzed off. Now he was really awake.

The fly buzzed widely about the room, but it was thinking of Charlie all the time. It swooped nearer and nearer. Nearer. . . .

Charlie pulled his head down under the bedclothes. All of him under the bedclothes, he was completely protected; but he could hear nothing except his heartbeats and his

172

DAVID McPHAIL DREW THESE PICTURES!

HE'S A VERY BUZZY ARTIST!

breathing. He was overwhelmed by the smell of warm bedding, warm pajamas, warm himself. He was going to suffocate. So he rose suddenly up out of the bedclothes; and the fly was waiting for him. It dashed at him. He beat at it with his hands. At the same time he appealed to his younger brother, Wilson, in the next bed, "Wilson, there's a fly!"

Wilson, unstirring, slept on.

Now Charlie and the fly were pitting their wits against each other: Charlie pouncing on the air where he thought the fly must be, the fly sliding under his guard towards his face. Again and again the fly reached Charlie; again and again, almost simultaneously, Charlie drove him away. Once he hit the fly—or, at least, hit where the fly had been a second before, on the side of his head; the blow was so hard that his head sang with it afterwards.

Then suddenly the fight was over; no more buzzing. His blows—or rather, one of them—must have told.

He laid his head back on the pillow, thinking of going to sleep again. But he was also thinking of the fly, and now he noticed a tickling in the ear he turned to the pillow.

It must be—it *was*—the fly.

He rose in such panic that the waking of Wilson really seemed to him a possible thing, and useful. He shook him repeatedly. "Wilson—Wilson, I tell you, there's a fly in my ear!"

Wilson groaned, turned over very slowly like a seal in water, and slept on.

The tickling in Charlie's ear continued. He could just imagine the fly struggling in some passageway too narrow for its wingspan. He longed to put his finger into his ear and rattle it around, like a stick in a rabbit hole; but he was afraid of driving the fly deeper into his ear.

Wilson slept on.

Charlie stood in the middle of the bedroom floor, quivering and trying to think. He needed to see down his ear, or to get someone else to see down it. Wilson wouldn't do; perhaps Margaret would.

Margaret's room was next door. Charlie turned on the light as he entered; Margaret's bed was empty. He was startled, and then thought that she must have gone to the bathroom. But there was no light from there. He listened carefully; there was no sound from anywhere, except for the usual snuffling moans from the hall, where Floss slept and dreamed of dog biscuits. The empty bed was mystifying, but Charlie had his ear to worry about. It sounded as if there were a pigeon inside it now.

Wilson asleep; Margaret vanished; that left Alison. But Alison was bossy, just because she was the eldest; and anyway she would probably only wake Mum. He might as well wake Mum himself.

Down the passage and through the door always left ajar. "Mum," he said.

She woke, or at least half-woke, at once. "Who is it? Who? Who? What's the matter? What?—"

"I've a fly in my ear."

"You can't have."

"It flew in."

She switched on the bedside light, and as she did so, Dad plunged beneath the bedclothes with an exclamation and lay still again.

Charlie knelt at his mother's side of the bed, and she looked into his ear. "There's nothing."

"Something crackles."

"It's wax in your ear."

"It tickles."

"There's no fly there. Go back to bed and stop imagining things."

His father's arm came up from below the bedclothes. The hand waved about, settled on the bedside light, and clicked it out. There was an upheaval of bedclothes and a comfortable grunt.

"Good night," said Mum from the darkness. She was already allowing herself to sink back into sleep again.

"Good night," Charlie said sadly. Then an idea occurred to him. He repeated his good night loudly and added some coughing, to cover the fact that he was closing the bedroom door behind him—the door that Mum kept open so that she could listen for her children. They had outgrown all that kind of attention, except possibly for Wilson. Charlie had shut the door against Mum's hearing because he intended to slip downstairs for a drink of water—well, for a drink and perhaps a snack. That fly business had woken him up and also weakened him; he needed something.

He crept downstairs, trusting to Floss's good sense not to make a row. He turned at the foot of the staircase towards the kitchen, and there had not been the faintest whimper from her, far less a bark. He was passing the dog basket when he had the most unnerving sensation of something being wrong there—something unusual, at least. He could not have said whether he had heard something or smelled some-

175

thing—he could certainly have seen nothing in the blackness; perhaps some extra sense warned him.

"Floss?" he whispered, and there was the usual little scrabble and snuffle. He held out his fingers low down for Floss to lick. As she did not do so at once, he moved them towards her, met some obstruction—

"Don't poke your fingers in my eye!" a voice said, very low-toned and cross. Charlie's first, confused thought was that Floss had spoken; the voice was familiar—but then a voice from Floss should *not* be familiar; it should be strangely new to him—

He took an uncertain little step towards the voice, tripped over the obstruction, which was quite wrong in shape and size to be Floss, and sat down. Two things now happened. Floss, apparently having climbed over the obstruc-

tion, reached his lap and began to lick his face. At the same time a human hand fumbled over his face, among the slappings of Floss's tongue, and settled over his mouth. "Don't make a row! Keep quiet!" said the same voice. Charlie's mind cleared; he knew, although without understanding, that he was sitting on the floor in the dark with Floss on his knee and Margaret beside him.

Her hand came off his mouth.

"What are you doing here anyway, Charlie?"

"I like that! What about you? There was a fly in my ear."

"Go on!"

"There was."

"Why does that make you come downstairs?"

"I wanted a drink of water."

"There's water in the bathroom."

"Well, I'm a bit hungry."

"If Mum catches you. . . "

"Look here," Charlie said, "you tell me what you're doing down here."

Margaret sighed. "Just sitting with Floss."

"You can't come down and just sit with Floss in the middle of the night."

"Yes, I can. I keep her company. Only at weekends, of course. No one seemed to realize what it was like for her when those puppies went. She just couldn't get to sleep for loneliness."

"But the last puppy went weeks ago. You haven't been keeping Floss company every Saturday night since then."

"Why not?"

Charlie gave up. "I'm going to get my food and drink," he said. He went into the kitchen, followed by Margaret, followed by Floss.

They all had a quick drink of water. Then Charlie and Margaret looked into the larder: there was a very large quantity of mashed potatoes; most of a loaf; eggs; butter; cheese . . .

"I suppose it'll have to be just bread and butter and a bit of cheese," said Charlie. "Else Mum might notice."

"Something hot," said Margaret. "I'm cold from sitting in the hall comforting Floss. I need hot cocoa, I think." She poured some milk into a saucepan and put it on the hot plate. Then she began a search for the cocoa. Charlie was already absorbed in the making of a rough cheese sandwich.

The milk in the pan began to steam. Given time, it rose in the saucepan, peered over the top, and boiled over onto the hot plate, where it sizzled loudly. Margaret rushed back and pulled the saucepan to one side. "Well, really, Charlie! Now there's that awful smell! It'll still be here in the morning, too."

"Set the fan going," Charlie suggested.

178

A LARDER IS
A COOL PLACE OR
A ROOM WHERE FOOD IS KEPT!

COOL WORD!

The fan drew the smell from the stove up and away through a pipe to the outside. It also made a loud roaring noise. Not loud enough to reach their parents, who slept on the other side of the house—that was all that Charlie and Margaret thought of.

Alison's bedroom, however, was immediately above the kitchen. Charlie was eating his bread and cheese, Margaret was drinking her cocoa, when the kitchen door opened and there stood Alison. Only Floss was pleased to see her.

"Well!" she said.

Charlie muttered something about a fly in his ear, but Margaret said nothing. Alison had caught them red-handed. She would call Mum downstairs, that was obvious. There would be an awful row.

Alison stood there. She liked commanding a situation.

Then, instead of taking a step backward to call up the stairs to Mum, she took a step forward into the kitchen.

"What are you having, anyway?" she asked. She glanced with scorn at Charlie's poor piece of bread and cheese and at Margaret's cocoa. She moved over to the larder, flung open the door, and looked searchingly inside. In such a way must Napoleon have viewed a battlefield before the victory.

Her gaze fell upon the bowl of mashed potatoes. "I shall make potato cakes," said Alison.

They watched while she brought the mashed potatoes to the kitchen table. She switched on the oven, fetched her other ingredients, and began mixing.

"Mum'll notice if you take much of those potatoes," said Margaret.

But Alison thought big. "She may notice if some potatoes are missing," she agreed. "But if there are none at all, and if the bowl they were in is washed and dried and stacked away with the others, then she's going to think she must have made a mistake. There just can never have been any mashed potatoes."

Alison rolled out her mixture and cut it into cakes; then she set the cakes on a baking tin and put it in the oven.

Now she did the washing up. Throughout the time they were in the kitchen, Alison washed up and put away as she went along. She wanted no one's help. She was very methodical, and she did everything herself to be sure that nothing was left undone. In the morning there must be no trace left of the cooking in the middle of the night.

"And now," said Alison, "I think we should fetch Wilson."

The other two were aghast at the idea, but Alison was firm in her reasons. "It's better if we're all in this together, Wilson as well. Then, if worst comes to worst, it won't be just us three caught out, with Wilson hanging on to Mum's apron

strings, smiling innocence. We'll all be in it together, and Mum'll be softer with us if we've got Wilson."

They saw that, at once. But Margaret still objected. "Wilson will tell. He just always tells everything. He can't help it."

Alison said, "He always tells everything. Right. We'll give him something *to* tell, and then see if Mum believes him. We'll put on a show for him. Get an umbrella from the hall and Wilson's sou'wester and a blanket or a rug or something. Go on."

They would not obey Alison's orders until they had heard her plan; then they did. They fetched the umbrella and the hat, and lastly they fetched Wilson, still sound asleep, slung between the two of them in his eiderdown. They propped him in a chair at the kitchen table, where he still slept.

By now the potato cakes were done. Alison took them out of the oven and set them on the table before Wilson. She buttered them, handing them in turn to Charlie and Margaret and helping herself. One was set aside to cool for Floss.

The smell of fresh-cooked, buttery potato cake woke Wilson, as was to be expected. First his nose sipped the air; then his eyes opened; his gaze settled on the potato cakes.

"Like one?" Alison asked.

Wilson opened his mouth wide, and Alison put a potato cake inside, whole.

"They're paradise cakes," Alison said.

"Potato cakes?" said Wilson, recognizing the taste.

"No, paradise cakes, Wilson," and then, stepping aside, she gave him a clear view of Charlie's and Margaret's show, with the umbrella and the sou'wester hat and his eiderdown. "Look, Wilson, look."

181

EIDERDOWN IS ANOTHER WORD FOR "QUILT"

IT'S BECAUSE THEY USED TO STUFF THE QUILTS WITH DOWN FROM EIDER DUCKS!

Wilson watched with wide-open eyes, and into his wide-open mouth Alison put, one by one, the potato cakes that were his share.

But, as they had foreseen, Wilson did not stay awake for long. When there were no more potato cakes, he yawned, drowsed, and suddenly was deeply asleep. Charlie and Margaret put him back into his eiderdown and took him upstairs to bed again. They came down to see Floss back into her basket. Alison, last out of the kitchen, made sure that everything was in its place.

The next morning Mum was down first. On Sunday she always cooked a proper breakfast for anyone there in time.

Dad was always there in time, but this morning Mum was still looking for a bowl of mashed potatoes when he appeared.

"I can't think where it's gone," she said. "I can't think."

"I'll have the bacon and eggs without the potatoes," said Dad; and he did. While he ate, Mum went back to searching.

Wilson came down, and was sent upstairs again to put on a robe. On his return he said that Charlie was still asleep and there was no sound from the girls' rooms either. He said he thought they were tired out. He went on talking while he ate his breakfast. Dad was reading the paper and Mum had gone back to poking about in the larder for the bowl of mashed potatoes, but Wilson liked talking even if no one would listen: ". . . and Charlie sat in an umbrella boat on an eiderdown sea, and Margaret pretended to be a sea serpent, and Alison gave us paradise cakes to eat. Floss had one too, but it was too hot for her. What are paradise cakes? Dad, what's a paradise cake?"

"Don't know," said Dad, reading.

"Mum, what's a paradise cake?"

"Oh, Wilson, don't bother me so when I'm looking for something. . . . When did you eat this cake, anyway?"

"I told you. Charlie sat in his umbrella boat on an eiderdown sea and Margaret was a sea serpent and Alison—"

"Wilson," said his mother, "you've been dreaming."

"No, really—really!" Wilson cried.

But his mother paid no further attention. "I give up," she said. "Those mashed potatoes; it must have been last weekend. . . ." She went out of the kitchen to call the others. "Charlie! Margaret! Alison!"

Wilson, in the kitchen, said to his father, "I wasn't dreaming. And Charlie said there was a fly in his ear."

Dad had been quarter-listening; now he put down his paper. "What?"

"Charlie had a fly in his ear."

Dad stared at Wilson. "And what did you say that Alison fed you with?"

"Paradise cakes. She'd just made them, I think, in the middle of the night."

"What were they like?"

"Lovely. Hot, with butter. Lovely."

"But were they—well, could they have had any mashed potatoes in them, for instance?"

In the hall Mum was finishing her calling. "Charlie! Margaret! Alison! I warn you now!"

"I don't know about that," Wilson said. "They were paradise cakes. They tasted a bit like the potato cakes Mum makes, but Alison said they weren't. She especially said they were paradise cakes."

Dad nodded. "You've finished your breakfast. Go up and get dressed, and you can take this"—he took a coin from his pocket—"straight off to the sweetshop. Go on."

Mum met Wilson at the kitchen door. "Where's he off to in such a hurry?"

"I gave him something to buy sweets with," said Dad. "I wanted a quiet breakfast. He talks too much."

THAT'S THE SILLIEST STORY I EVER READ!

I LOVED IT! THAT FAMILY MUST BE A LOT OF FUN!

184

I Heard A Bird Sing

by Oliver Herford

I heard a bird sing
    In the dark of December,
A magical thing
    And sweet to remember.
"We are nearer to Spring
    Than we were in September,"
I heard a bird sing
    In the dark of December.

Cedar Waxwing drawn by Eva Hülsmann

TONGUE

Try to say each of these tongue twisters five times in a row, as fast as you can! Start with:

Peggy Babcock.

Is your tongue all twisted in knots? Mine is! Peggy Babcock is one of the hardest tongue twisters in the English language! Here's an easier one:

A critical cricket critic.

And some more for practice ... remember – five times, FAST!

Tim, the thin twin tinsmith.

LADYBUG
LIKES LICKING
LACY LIGHT
LAYER CAKE

Drawing by Trina Hyman

TWISTERS

COLLECTED BY ALVIN SCHWARTZ

Does this shop stock short socks with spots?

Tom threw Tim three thumbtacks.

'Lisbeth lisps lengthy lessons.

Slim Sam slid sideways.

The dude dropped in at the Dewdrop Inn.

Rubber baby buggy bumpers.

A black-backed bath brush.

Floating Frankfurter

by Martin Gardner

To see this curious optical illusion, first place the tips of your index fingers together, holding them about three inches in front of your eyes as shown. Look *past* the fingers, focusing your eyes on something in the distance.

Now separate the tips of your fingers about half an inch. You'll see a sausage-shaped finger, with a nail at each end, floating, all by itself, in the air between your fingertips!

This is what happens. By focusing on a distant point, you prevent the separate images of your finger (one image in each eye) from coming together. Your left eye's image of your left finger and your right eye's image of your right finger overlap to form the solid-looking frankfurter that seems to be floating in space.

IS IT WORKING FOR YOU, CRICKET?

IT'S HARD TO TELL! I DON'T SEE A FRANKFU BUT I DO SEE A STRA FLOATING BLACK TW

Drawing by Trina Schart Hyman

A Picnic with the Aunts
by Ursula Moray Williams

There were once six lucky, lucky boys who were invited by their aunts to go on a picnic expedition to an island in the middle of a lake.

The boys' names were Freddie, Adolphus, Edward, Montague, Montmorency, and little John Henry. Their aunts were Aunt Bossy, Aunt Millicent, Aunt Celestine, Aunt Miranda, Aunt Adelaide, and Auntie Em.

The picnic was to be a great affair, since the lake was ten miles away, and they were to drive there in a wagon pulled by two gray horses. Once arrived at the lake, they were to leave the wagon and get into a rowboat with all the provisions for the picnic, including umbrellas, in case it rained. The aunts were bringing a bat and balls for the boys to

HE'S COMING ALL THE WAY FROM LONDON, TO OUR PICNIC!

FRITZ WEGNER DREW THESE FUNNY AND BEAUTIFUL PICTURES!

WHO ARE YOU?

WE'RE THE ANTS! MY NAME IS MARIANNE AND THIS IS MY SISTER ANNA!

... YOU CAN'T HAVE A PICNIC WITHOUT ANTS!

189

play with, and a rope for them to jump over. There was also a box of fireworks to shoot off at the close of the day when it was getting dark, before they all got into the boat and rowed back to the shore. The wagon with Davy Driver would leave them at the lake in the morning and come back to fetch them in the evening, at nine o'clock.

The food for the picnic was out of this world, for all the aunts were excellent cooks. There were strawberry tarts made by Aunt Bossy, and gingerbread covered with almonds baked by Aunt Millicent. Aunt Celestine had prepared dozens of sausage rolls, while Aunt Miranda's cheese tarts were packed in a tea cozy to keep them warm. Aunt Adelaide had made so many sandwiches, they had to be packed in a suitcase, while Auntie Em had supplied soda pop and apples, each one polished like a looking glass on the back of her best skirt.

Besides the provisions, the aunts had brought their embroidery and their knitting, a book of fairy tales in case the boys were tired, a bottle of medicine in case they were ill, and a cane in case they were naughty. And they had invited the boys' headmaster from school, Mr. Hamm, to join the party, as company for themselves and to prevent their nephews from becoming too unruly.

The wagon called for the boys at nine o'clock in the morning—all the aunts were wearing their best Sunday hats, and the boys had been forced by their mother into their best sailor suits. When Headmaster Hamm had been picked up, the party was complete, only he had brought his fiddle with him and the wagon was really overcrowded. At each hill the boys had to get out and walk, which they considered very unfair, for their headmaster was so fat, he must have weighed far more than the six of them put together. But they arrived at the lake at last.

There was a great unpacking of aunts and provisions, a repetition of orders to Davy Driver, and a scolding of little boys, who were running excitedly toward the water's edge with knitting wool wound around their ankles.

A large rowboat was moored to a ring on the shore. When it was loaded with passengers and provisions, it was even more overcrowded than the wagon had been, but Aunt Bossy seized an oar and Headmaster Hamm another—Auntie Em took a third, while two boys manned each of the remaining three.

Amid much splashing and screaming, the boat moved slowly away from the shore and inched across the lake to the distant island, the boys crashing their oars together while Auntie Em and Aunt Bossy grew pinker and pinker in the face as they strove to keep up with Headmaster Hamm, who rowed in his shirt sleeves, singing the "Volga Boat Song."

It was a hot summer's day. The lake lay like a sheet of glass, except for the long ragged wake behind the boat. Since they all were rowing with their backs to the island, they hit it long before they realized they had arrived, and the jolt crushed Aunt Millicent's legs between the strawberry tarts and the soda pop bottles.

The strawberry jam oozed onto her shins, convincing her that she was bleeding to death. She lay back fainting in the arms of Headmaster Hamm, until little John Henry remarked that Aunt Millicent's blood looked just like his favorite jam, whereupon she immediately sat up and told him that he was a very disgusting little boy.

Aunt Bossy decided that the boat should be tied up in the

shade of some willow trees and the provisions left inside it to keep cool until dinnertime. The boys were very disappointed, for they were all hungry and thought it must be long past dinnertime already.

"You boys can go and play," Aunt Bossy told them. She gave them the bat and balls, and the rope to jump over, but they did not want to jump or play ball. They wanted to rush about the island and explore, to look for birds' nests and climb trees, to play cowboys and swim in the lake.

But all the aunts began to make aunt-noises at once:

"Don't get too hot!"

"Don't get too cold!"

"Don't get dirty!"

"Don't get wet!"

"Keep your hats on or you'll get sunstroke!"

"Keep your shoes on or you'll cut your feet!"

"Keep out of the water or you'll be drowned!"

"Don't fight!"

"Don't shout!"

"Be good!"

"Be good!"

"Be good!"

"There! You hear what your aunts say," added Headmaster Hamm. "So mind you are good!"

The six aunts and Headmaster Hamm went to sit under the trees to knit and embroider and play the fiddle, leaving the boys standing on the shore, looking gloomily at one another.

"Let's not be good," said Adolphus.

"But if we aren't," said Edward, "we won't get any dinner."

"Let's have dinner first," suggested little John Henry.

They sat down on the grass above the willow trees, looking down on the boat. It was a long time since breakfast, and they could not take their eyes off the boxes of provisions tucked underneath the seats, the bottles of pop restored to order, and Auntie Em's basket of shining, rosy apples.

Voices came winging across the island:

"Why are you boys sitting there doing nothing at all? Why can't you find something nice to do on this lovely island?"

Quite coldly and firmly Freddie stood up and faced his brothers.

"Shall we leave them to it?" he suggested.

"What do you mean?" cried Adolphus, Edward, Montague, Montmorency, and little John Henry.

"We'll take the boat and the provisions and row away to the other end of the lake, leaving them behind!" said Freddie calmly.

"Leave them behind on the island!" his brothers echoed faintly.

As the monstrous suggestion sank into their minds, all six boys began to picture the fun they might have if they were free of the aunts and Headmaster Hamm. As if in a dream they followed Freddie to the boat, stepped inside, and cast off the rope. At the very last moment Adolphus flung the suitcase of sandwiches ashore before each boy seized an oar and rowed for their lives away from the island.

By the time the six aunts and Headmaster Hamm had realized what was happening, the boat was well out into the lake, and the boys took not the slightest notice of the waving handkerchiefs, the calls, the shouts, the pleadings, and even the bribes that followed them across the water.

It was a long, hard pull to the end of the lake, but not a boy gave up until the bow of the boat touched shore and the island was a blur in the far distance. Then, rubbing the blistered palms of their hands, they jumped ashore, tying the boat to a rock and tossing the provisions from one to another in a willing chain.

Then began the most unforgettable afternoon of their lives. It started with a feast, when each boy stuffed himself with whatever he fancied most. Pop bottles popped and fizzed; apple cores were tossed far and wide. When they had finished eating, they amused themselves by writing impolite little messages to their aunts and to Headmaster Hamm, stuffing them into the empty bottles, and sending them off in the direction of the island.

They wrote such things as:

Hey diddle diddle
Old Hamm and his fiddle—
Sharp at both ends
And flat in the middle!

Aunt Miranda has got so thin
She has got nothing to keep her inside in.

My Aunt Boss rides a hoss.
Which is boss, hoss or Boss?

Fortunately, since they forgot to replace the tops, all the bottles filled with water and sank to the bottom long before they reached their goal.

After this the boys swam in the lake, discovering enough mud and weeds to plaster themselves with dirt until they looked like savages. Drying themselves on the trousers of their sailor suits, they dressed again and ran up into the hills beyond the lake where they discovered a cave and spent an enchanting afternoon playing robbers and hurling great stones down the steep hillside.

196

Feeling hungry again, the boys ate the rest of the provisions, and then, too impatient to wait for the dark, decided to shoot off the box of fireworks. Even by daylight these provided a splendid exhibition as Freddie lit one after another. Then a spark fell on Montague's collar, burning a large hole, while Montmorency burned his hand and hopped about crying loudly. To distract him, Freddie lit the largest rocket of all, which they had been keeping for the last.

They all waited breathlessly for it to go off, watching the little red spark creep slowly up the twist of paper until it reached the vital spot. With a tremendous hiss the rocket shot into the air. Montmorency stopped sucking his hand, and all the boys cheered.

But the rocket hesitated and faltered in midflight. It turned a couple of somersaults in the air and dived straight into the boat, landing in the bow with a crash.

Before it could burn the wood or do any damage, Freddie rushed after it. With a prodigious bound he leaped into the boat that had drifted a few yards from the shore.

Unfortunately he landed so heavily that his foot went right through one of the boards, and although he seized the stick of the rocket and hurled it far into the lake, the water came through the hole so quickly that the fire would have been quenched in any case.

There was nothing that any of them could do, for the boat was rotten, and the plank had simply given way. They were forced to stand and watch it sink before their eyes in four feet of water.

The sun was setting now. The surrounding hills threw blue shadows into the lake. A little breeze sprang up ruffling the water. The island seemed infinitely far away.

Soberly, sadly, the six boys began to walk down the shore to the beginning of the lake, not knowing what they would do when they got there. They were exhausted by their long, mad afternoon—some were crying and others limping.

Secretly the younger ones hoped that when they arrived they would find the grown-ups waiting for them, but when they reached the beginning of the lake, no grown-ups were there. Not even Davy Driver.

"We will build a fire!" Freddie announced to revive their spirits. "It will keep us warm and show our aunts we are all safe and well."

"They get so anxious about us!" said Montmorency.

So they built an enormous bonfire from all the driftwood and dry branches they could find. This cheered them all very much because they were strictly forbidden to make bonfires at home.

It was dark by now, but they had the fire for light, and suddenly the moon rose, full and stately, flooding the lake with a sheet of silver. The boys laughed and shouted. They flung more branches onto the fire and leaped up and down.

198

THESE BOYS ARE BEING VERY BAD ARENT THEY?

I THINK IT SOUNDS LIKE A LOT OF FUN!

WHEN THEIR MOTHER FINDS OUT, I'LL BET IT WONT BE MUCH FUN!

Suddenly Adolphus stopped in midair and pointed, horror-struck, toward the water.

Far out on the silver lake, sharply outlined against the moonlight, they saw a sight that froze their blood to the marrow. It was the aunts' hats, drifting toward the shore.

The same little breeze that rippled the water and fanned their fire was blowing the six hats away from the island, and as they floated closer and closer to the shore, the boys realized for the first time what a terrible thing they had done, for kind Aunt Bossy, generous Aunt Millicent, good Aunt Celestine, devoted Aunt Miranda, worthy Aunt Adelaide, and dear, *dear* Auntie Em, together with their much respected headmaster, Mr. Hamm, had all been *drowned!*

Freddie, Adolphus, Edward, Montague, Montmorency, and little John Henry burst into tears of such genuine repentance and grief that it would have done their aunts good to hear them. They sobbed so bitterly, that after a while they had no more tears left to weep, and it was little John Henry who first wiped his eyes on his sleeve and recovered his composure. The next moment his mouth opened wide and his eyes seemed about to burst out of his head.

He pointed a trembling finger toward the lake, and all his brothers looked where he was pointing. Then their eyes

CAN YOU SWIM, ANNA? ..... YES, MARIANNE— ALL AUNTS CAN SWIM!

HOW DO THEY EVER FIND BATHING SUITS TINY ENOUGH TO FIT THEM?

bulged, too, and their mouths dropped open as they beheld the most extraordinary sight they had ever dreamed of.

The aunts were swimming home!

For under the hats there were heads, and behind the heads small wakes of foam bore witness to the efforts of the swimmers.

The hats were perfectly distinguishable. First came Aunt Bossy's blue hydrangeas, topped by a purple bow, then Aunt Millicent's little lilac bonnet. Close behind Aunt Millicent came Aunt Celestine's straw hat, smartly ribboned in green plush, followed by Aunt Miranda's black velvet cap with a bunch of violets. Then some yards farther from the shore a floral platter of pansies and roses that Aunt Adelaide had bought to open a church bazaar. And last of all came Auntie Em in her pink straw pillbox hat, dragging behind her with a rope the picnic suitcase, on which was seated Headmaster Hamm, who could not swim.

Holding the sides of the suitcase very firmly with both hands, he carried between his teeth, as a dog carries a most important bone, the aunts' cane.

Motionless and petrified with terror and relief, Freddie, Adolphus, Edward, Montague, Montmorency, and little John Henry stood on the shore—the fire shining on their filthy suits, dirty faces, and sodden shoes, while slowly, steadily the aunts swam back from the island, and far behind them over the hills appeared at last the lights of Davy Driver's wagon, coming to fetch them home.

No More Woxes

A Short Tall Tale by Ruth Krauss

There was a wolf
and there was a fox and
they ate each other up.
And that made the wox.

Then the wox
ate himself up and
that's why there are
no more woxes.

MAURICE SENDAK
DREW THE
WOXES!

SHALL WE
INVITE HIM
TO OUR PICNIC?

NO, HE'S TOO BUSY!

At Fish for Finn

by Eve Bunting

Finn McCool was the only giant in all Ireland, and a terrible good one he was, too. He lived in the town of Dunmill with his wife, Oonagh, and the people thereabouts thought very well of him.

When it was time for a man to put new thatch on his roof, he knew who to call on for help. Big as Finn was, he could stand on the ground and do the thatching with no need of a ladder.

If a horse needed shoeing, Finn worked with the blacksmith, lifting the beast clear off the ground so the work could be done with no fuss or bother.

When the fishing boats set out of a windless morning, Finn waded waist deep in the Irish sea, pushing two before him and pulling two behind, tied to his belt. The sorrow of it was that he could never go fishing with the rest of them, for there wasn't a boat built that could carry him. And when the salmon ran fat in the deep River Boyne, all the men of Dunmill angled and trolled from the green grassy banks, all ex-

202

OUR OLD FRIEND ENRICO ARNO DID THESE ILLUSTRATIONS!

HE'S BRINGING THE WINE TO OUR PICNIC!

cept Finn McCool. Finn stayed home or came to watch, for his hands were too big to hold a rod, and the rod he could hold was too big for the fish. It was a sad circumstance altogether, and he longed and he longed for a fish of his own.

One morning, very early, Oonagh heard a knocking at her front door. Finn was still snoring in the bed beside her, his two big feet sticking clear out of the bedroom window. When Finn built their house, he had measured himself standing up, for he knew he'd have to fit. But he'd forgotten entirely that he'd need to lie down. Finn did things like that. But then, as the people of the town always said, a man can't have everything. "Finn's as good a big fellow as ever wore a hat," they said, "and sure if his brains don't match his size, what matter? We'll take care of him."

Rat-tat-tat. Oonagh heard the knocking on her door again. She slipped out of bed carefully, not to waken Finn. Michael Mor, the village baker, stood on the step.

"God bless all here," he said, taking off his cap and making a little bow. "I've come for himself, but I can hear he's sleeping."

Oonagh smiled. "Aye. He has a fine pair of lungs in him. You could hear him in Cork if you'd a mind to it."

Michael Mor could hardly stand still. "A giant salmon's been spotted in the river!" he squeaked with excitement. "The biggest fish seen by man since the minds of any of us can remember."

"You do say!"

Michael Mor nodded. "He has a hooked snout and a humped back, and he's six foot if he's an inch. We none of us made to catch him, for sure there wasn't a man there with a line fit to hold him. No, nor six of us with the strength to pull him in." He stopped for breath. "Anyways, we were thinking, the fish by rights should belong to Finn. He's our only giant, and a good one he is. This is one salmon he could take with his own line and hook."

They looked at each other, and Oonagh smiled. "A fish of his own! I'm thanking you, Michael Mor."

They listened and heard the silence. Oonagh looked at the bedroom window. The snoring had stopped, and the two big feet were gone.

"Where is this fish?" Finn stood behind Oonagh. He was

dressed, and he carried his fishing pole made from the topmost branch of a sycamore tree. His line was a mooring rope, the line that had never taken a fish. "Where is this salmon?"

"He's headed upstream and he's headed fast," Michael Mor shouted. "But sure with the legs you have on you, Finn, you could be in Ballyblae before him and awaiting his pleasure."

"I'm off!" Finn set his fishing hat on his head. "I'm obliged to you, Michael. Wife, get a good fire going. There'll be fish for supper."

Then he was gone. Two big steps took him down the hill. Two more took him through the town of Dunmill, the thunder of his feet cracking the whitewash on the cottages. He stepped over a bridge, over a windmill, over a mountain where sheep grazed, and saw before him the roofs of Ballyblae.

There he stopped where the Boyne ran clear and deep, the pebbles on the bottom brown and speckled as thrush eggs. He took from his pocket a round red cheese and a hook the size of a ship's anchor. The shadow of him spread dark on the water, and he remembered what the fishermen made him do when he went with them. He lay the length of himself on the riverbank and stuck the round red cheese on the end of the hook. Then he dropped his line and let the current have it. The cheese bobbed like a football.

Finn put his hat beneath his head and lay still, waiting. The sky and the fields and the river were empty. Except . . . except for a shadow that came sliding and gliding along the bottom of the Boyne.

Finn held his breath. In that instant he saw the fish, and it was bigger than he had known a fish could be. He saw the silver sheen of it and the big hooked snout of it and the eyes like two glass bowls of currant jelly. He saw that the eyes

were on the round red cheese and that the mouth was open
and ready. The salmon bit and Finn leaped up, pulling the
line from the water. The fish was not on the hook. Neither
was the round red cheese.

"You stole it, so you did," Finn roared. "You stole my
round red cheese!" He took the hook from the line and
blundered into the river, holding it in his hand. "I thought
I'd caught me a fish of my own, but you tricked me, so you
did." He hacked at the river with the hook, laying about
himself like a thresher with a scythe. "Begorrah, I'll get you,
if I have to empty the river to do it!"

He saw a flash of silver between his feet, and he brought
the hook down and felt it catch on something soft and firm,
and he lifted the hook from the water and saw the fish
speared on the barb. The river streamed from the silver
sides, and the salmon flashed and thrashed so that the Boyne
itself seemed to scatter and scream.

Finn raised the hook high in the air. "I've got you. The
first fish of my own, and a right looking one you are."

The fish hung motionless, a shining kite on a windless
day.

Finn brought it down and took it in his hands, and they
studied each other face to face. Finn saw where the hook
went into the fish's neck, and he was sorry. "Stay still," he
said. "I had no mind to hurt you, though isn't that the silly
thing to be saying, and me making to take you home for my

supper? I'll have this wicked thing out of you in a minute. There's nothing in my heart says you have to be suffering." He held the fish in one hand and worked at the hook with the other.

The eyes of the big salmon grew dull and cloudy.

"Are you dead already?" Finn asked, and he felt a terrible sorrow, for he was a good and gentle man, and this was the first living creature he had ever in his life harmed. "There's a difference, I'm thinking, to salmon on a plate and salmon in the river. Sure if I was a fishing man, I'd lose my appetite for the stuff entirely."

He had to twist the hook to free it, and he had to tug, and it came loose with a jerk, the end of it catching itself in Finn's own thumb.

"Ow!" He leaped in the air at the sharpness of the pain.

"Pull it out, man. Pull it out."

Finn was so surprised that he stopped yelping and jumping. "You can *speak*?"

"Aye," the salmon said. "And you'd better take that thing from your thumb, for it's a desperate weapon altogether. And I'm the one that knows it!"

Finn looked at the fish and saw the wound in its neck, and he looked at his thumb and saw the bright blood oozing around the hook. "Ow, ow!" He danced a little pain jig.

"Take it out, man!" The salmon's voice was impatient.

"But sure I have no free hand."

"That's true. You'd better put me back in the Boyne, for I'm thinking now you have need of that hand for more than holding me."

Finn dropped the salmon and saw the river open and cover it with the comfort of its waters. He sat on the riverbank and worked on the barb in his thumb and whimpered a

bit, for though he was bigger than anybody else, he wasn't
any braver. He twisted and jerked and the barb came free.

"Suck your thumb now," the salmon called from the
river. "It'll be all right so."

Finn put his thumb in his mouth and felt the pleasure of
his own warmth on the hurt, and all at once he knew things
he'd never known before. He knew how birds flew and how
fishes swam and how men thought and what kept the stars in
the sky and the names of every one of them from the
smallest to the largest. He was dizzy with knowledge. He
took his thumb from his mouth and the world steadied.

The salmon swam in widening arcs. "I should be telling

GEORGE, DO YOU THINK FISHING IS A CRUEL SPORT?

ONLY WHEN THEY USE WORMS FOR BAIT!

you that I'm not only the biggest salmon in the world, I'm also the smartest salmon in the world," he said.

Finn shook his head. There was no way he could understand the things that were happening.

"You see, Finn McCool, you live with friends, and there's nobody yet has sought to harm you. Me, now, the bigger I got, the more men tried to catch me. So I got smarter. Too smart for them."

"I caught you," Finn said.

"Aye!" The fish curved in two wings of creamy water. "But I've never met up with a giant before, swinging a hook like a madman. It's a wonder you didn't scare the senses right out of me."

"I'm regretting that, salmon."

"I know you are. You put the barb in my neck, but the eyes of you and the hands of you were full of sorrow, after. And remember, giant, you were smart enough to catch me but not smart enough to keep me. You could as easily have put me on the bank as back in the river. I'd be in your pocket this minute and ready for the pan." The fish sighed. "You're a good man, Finn, but I'm thinking your brains leave a lot wanting. And that won't do. Big isn't enough, for the day may come when you meet up with an enemy who's bigger than you and smarter than you, too. So I'm bequeathing a gift to you. That thumb of yours, the one where our two bloods mixed, will be your wisdom thumb from this day on. When you have a need to know where the wind comes from or what makes the river run or the name of every king in Ireland since time began, suck on your thumb. The wisdom's there and waiting."

Finn looked at his big ugly thumb with the gash across the breadth of it. "You do say!"

"Good-bye to you then, Finn McCool. Thanks for the cheese. And don't be worrying yourself about my sore neck. I heal fast."

Finn watched as the waters opened for the big salmon and closed behind him. "Now *why* did I put him back in the river?" he asked himself. "I'm a gormless creature, so I am!" He put his thumb in his mouth to ease the hurt, and he knew about the fish and about himself. Smart he was not and never had been, but he cared about people and about creatures. He had known when he saw the fish face to face, that he couldn't kill it, or any living thing. He had known that giants are few, be they fish or man, and rare enough to be left alone. These things he understood with his heart, not his mind. It was almost enough.

Finn shouldered his rod, tucked his thumb in his belt for the day he might need it, and stepped over the mountain where the sheep grazed, over the windmill, over the bridge, through the town of Dunmill, and up the hill, home.

Shooting Stars
Herbert S. Zim

Dusk fell on November 12, 1833, as on any normal autumn evening. But as the constellation Orion, at first low in the east, climbed slowly higher and higher, people noticed shooting stars in the eastern sky. Soon so many were seen that people woke their neighbors to come to share this novel spectacle. Within a few hours the sky was ablaze with thousands of shooting stars, coming from the direction of the constellation Leo, the lion.

A rain of shooting stars, a shower of flashing light, spread over the entire sky—so awesome that people could scarcely believe their eyes. Wherever the night was clear, they marveled at the sight.

Illustrated by Jim Arnosky

Many fell on their knees to pray; others feared the world was ending. Church bells were rung. People crowded the streets, afraid to remain at home. Only with the dawn did the flashes of light fade away.

As the sun rose, fear died, and people began to realize that what they had seen was the greatest shower of shooting stars in history. Many showers have appeared since, but none as rich or as brilliant.

You, of course, have seen shooting or falling stars. Perhaps, as one flashed across the sky, a friend has said, "Make a wish." Or you may have heard your grandmother say, as one rapidly faded, "Someone has died." For a long time no one knew what shooting stars really were, so people believed such stories.

Shooting stars are more correctly called meteors. Meteors are only seen when they enter the earth's atmosphere, blaze

up, and burn out. Some meteors strike the earth and, when found, are called meteorites; so meteorites are fallen meteors.

Even before the great shower of 1833, astronomers had begun to study meteors. In 1798 two Germans compared observations and estimated that meteors were about 50 miles up—much higher than people had suspected. Until that time, people thought that meteors flashed a few miles away, like lightning. In 1803 a French scientist proved that meteorites were the same as meteors, and did come from outside the earth.

This idea was not easy to accept. A few years later President Thomas Jefferson, a scientist himself, heard that two professors had found a meteorite in western Connecticut. But he was skeptical. "I could more easily believe that two Yankee professors would lie," he is supposed to have said, "than that stones would fall from Heaven."

In recent years, scientists have proved that the flashes of light you see at night are caused by bits of iron or stone burning up as they hit the outer edge of the earth's atmosphere at great speed. The particles vary in size, in speed, and in composition. The light flashes they make also vary greatly.

The brightest meteors are called fireballs. These light up the entire sky and are seen for hundreds of miles. The ordinary meteors are much fainter—about as bright as a star. And as with the stars, there are many more faint ones that can only be seen with a telescope.

People do not see many meteors, mainly because they are not looking for them. But astronomers who watch the skies see them often. On a clear, average moonless night, you can see about 10 meteors an hour, watching only a small fraction of the total sky, and seeing only the brightest meteors. But

your rate of 10 an hour means a million an hour for the entire sky, or about 24 million meteors daily. Of these millions of meteors, 99.9% are no bigger than particles of dust.

Though millions of meteorites hit the earth's atmosphere each year, fewer than 2000 have been found and put in museums. Undoubtedly many more large meteorites have been lost in the ocean or in wilderness areas.

Records over the past century suggest that about 25 large meteorites fall in the United States each year. For the whole earth the total is about 2000—an average of perhaps 5 or 6 a day. Some of these meteorites weigh only a few ounces. The largest one found weighs over 60 tons.

In spite of the number of meteorites which fall, nobody has ever been killed by one. However, in November, 1954, a woman became the first human being known to be struck by one. She was bruised and badly scared. A few meteorites have hit houses. One hit a car. Many have been seen to fall, and some have been found within minutes after they struck the earth.

When a meteor enters the thin, upper atmosphere, it is moving so fast that it compresses the air ahead, raising the temperature to several thousand degrees. This heat melts the meteor's surface, changing it to glass if it is a stony meteor, or coating it with black iron oxide if it is an iron ore. Spattering droplets of white-hot liquid burn, and make the bright flash and glowing trail. Occasionally a noise like thunder is reported.

WE'LL HAVE A BARBECUE!

GOSH CRICKET WHAT SHALL WE DO IF A METEOR FALLS ON OUR PICNIC?

The brightness of meteors depends on their speed (faster ones are usually brighter), and on their weight.

The largest meteorites found are iron ones. Stony meteorites are usually smaller. Possibly because they are not as strong as iron, they break more easily in plunging through the air.

Meteorites striking the earth are buried, shattered, or lost, depending on their size and where they strike. When huge meteorites hit the earth, they may cause explosions as large as atomic bombs. A huge meteor has tremendous energy of motion. On striking the earth this great energy is changed instantly into heat. Heat vaporizes water in the soil and rock so fast that it causes a gigantic steam explosion.

In Arizona, near Winslow, is the best-known meteor crater in the United States. Here a great meteorite or swarm of meteorites struck at least 5000 years ago. The crater is almost circular—4200 feet across and 570 feet deep.

Most meteorites fall into two distinct classes—the stony and the iron, and it is a real possibility that both types were produced by the breaking up of a planet as large as the earth. The origin of large meteors may have been the greatest collision of all times within the solar system.

Meteorites are an important challenge to our imagination. Curiosity about flashes of light in the night sky and about odd stones has raised scores of questions. Many are not yet answered, but more and more people have joined the search. For to know the complete story of shooting stars, one must solve the mysteries of the solar system and of our entire universe as well. That is something to think about the next time you see a meteor.

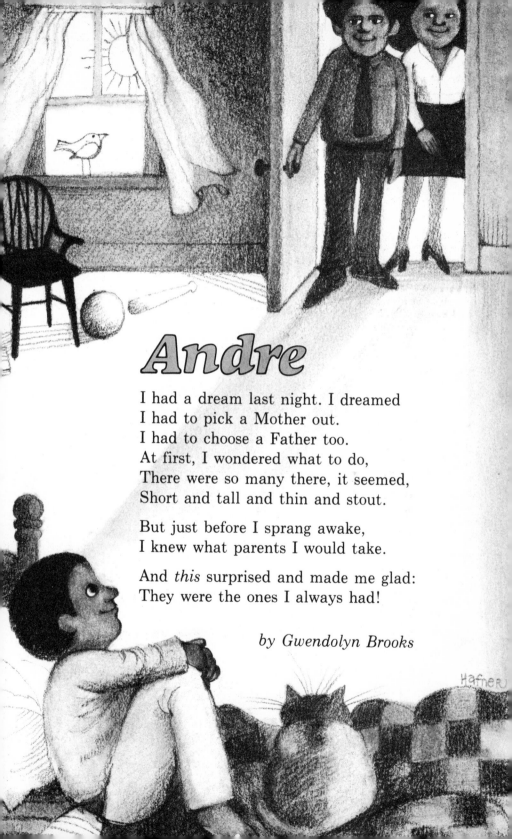

Andre

I had a dream last night. I dreamed
I had to pick a Mother out.
I had to choose a Father too.
At first, I wondered what to do,
There were so many there, it seemed,
Short and tall and thin and stout.

But just before I sprang awake,
I knew what parents I would take.

And *this* surprised and made me glad:
They were the ones I always had!

by Gwendolyn Brooks

CRICKET CAPERS

by Eddie Creech

Can you do this?

Put your hands behind your neck and rock on your tummy like a seesaw?

Can you wrap your arms around your legs and rock on your seat like a rocking chair?

Can you turn a somersault without falling over sideways?
Can you turn a somersault backwards?

Can you do a cartwheel with your legs flying over your head?

218

Drawings by Karen Gundersheimer

Can you sit with your legs and arms folded?

Can you walk blindfolded into another room without bumping into anything?

Can you do this?

Wiggle your ears without making a funny face?

Can you touch the floor with your fingers without bending your knees?

I COULD DO IT EASY IF I ONLY HAD FINGERS!

Or can you clasp your hands behind your back?
  That is easy.

All of these things you can do alone or with somebody else.
Of course, it is more fun to do them with someone else.

Can you do this?
  Jump in the air and touch your toes?

Can you stand on your head by balancing your body with your hands?

Can you say the alphabet? Say the alphabet backwards?

Can you jump in the air and click your heels? More than once? More than twice? You are an expert if you can.

Do you think you can tie a shoelace? Tie it faster than you can put on a shoe?

Can you hop on one leg? How many hops can you hop without falling down?

Can you sit perfectly still for ten minutes? That is not easy. But it can be done.

Some of these things you will not be able to do. Which ones?

FLORABEL and THE FABULOUS FLEA CIRCUS
by Eleanor Estes

nce there was a flea named Florabel. She was a ballerina flea and the star performer in the fabulous flea circus of Professor Fabadessa in the Tivoli Gardens in Copenhagen, Denmark.

"Here she comes! Here she comes!" the children would scream when Florabel made her grand entrance at the opening of the show, a lovely leap from the wings of the stage. "There she is! There she is!" and they would try to focus their opera glasses on Florabel, the favorite flea of the great circus.

It was hard to keep track of Florabel—she performed with such grace and rapidity. "I see her!" the children would gasp, for it was breathtaking to watch Florabel dance upon

BJÖRN BERG DID THESE DRAWINGS, LADYBUG!

HOW DO YOU SAY "BE MY VALENTINE" IN SWEDISH?

ISNT FLORABEL BEAUTIFUL!

IS A "POUND OF STERLING" THE SAME AS A POUND OF COOKIES?   NO, LADYBUG! IT'S ENGLISH MONEY!

WHAT'S A PAS DE DEUX?   IT'S FRENCH, AND IN BALLET IT MEANS A DANCE FOR TWO PEOPLE.

the high tightrope. Sometimes she rode a miniature bicycle up there and pirouetted upon the handlebars. This part of her performance usually ended with her astonishing leap to her golden trapeze.

It was for this leap that Florabel was most renowned, for it outdistanced all leaps recorded so far in flea-circus history. No one wanted to miss seeing that leap. If there are ever Olympic games for fleas, she will easily win all the gold medals in the leaping class.

No wonder the children would scarcely watch the other great performers of the flea circus, including the Grand Mogul, a magician from the Far East, or Signor Pellegrini, the weight lifter, who had come last year from Naples where they also have fine fleas. He had performed in many flea circuses throughout the world and in London had once lifted a pound sterling.

Far from being jealous of Florabel and her popularity, all the fleas of the circus were proud of her. Every bravo she received, every cheer that greeted her *pas de deux,* her graceful leap, her spin like a frenzied snowflake, gladdened

223

the hearts of all the performers, especially of the great flea Signor Pellegrini, who loved her dearly.

"Our little Princess! Our little Princess Florabel!" they all thought and stood respectfully aside as she took bow after bow after bow and blew kisses.

Florabel was the only member of the flea circus who had royal blood in her veins and could rightly be called "Princess." This is the way it came about.

One day the King of Denmark and the Prince, his seven-year-old son, rode to the Tivoli Gardens, as they often did, the King on his black horse named Dandy, the Prince on his pony named Paint. They came to see the sights, to hear the concert, to ride the little train, and finally to watch Professor Fabadessa's fabulous flea circus.

The Prince liked to play the game of "finding Florabel" as much as all the other children. He always hoped he would be the first to spot her. On this day, he was. "There she is!" he exclaimed when he saw her leap from her golden trapeze to the topmast of a Yankee Clipper that was drawn on stage by a single flea, Signor Pellegrini, of course.

"Ah-h-h!" gasped the delighted audience, for indeed there was Florabel, waving, rocking back and forth as though the ship were asea, and blowing kisses right and left. Suddenly Florabel stood poised, as still as a bird about to take wing. People knew she was about to make her famous leap. They carefully kept their opera glasses focused on her.

But Florabel, aloft upon the mast, had spotted the King and the Prince in the audience, and Florabel was a rather mischievous flea. She had always wanted to bite a royal person. Now was her chance, for the King had pushed the little Prince into the front line and was standing near him, but to the side where he wouldn't obstruct the view. The distance between Florabel and the King was great. But Florabel was a great artist. Here was her chance to bite a king and, at the same time, surpass her own record of long distance leaps. So she leaped!

With perfect timing and precision Florabel leaped into the left ear of the King of Denmark! It was the most dazzling leap of her life, so dazzling no one could see where it had landed her. People frantically adjusted their opera glasses, but no one could spot her. Even the King was puzzled and scratched his ear. And some people trying to attract attention to themselves said, "I saw her! I saw her!" Then they shriveled down into their collars, withered by the scorn heaped on them. "That's not Florabel! That's Molly!"

Molly was a Brooklyn flea—not bad as a performer, but far from Florabel's class. In fact, she was rather clumsy. However, Molly had a good brain, and she informed Signor Pellegrini that Florabel had leaped offstage but she didn't know where to. Signor Pellegrini knew, though, for he had the eyes of a hawk, having once bitten one near the Bay of Biscayne. Since he rarely took these hawk eyes off his beloved Florabel, he alone had spotted her as she landed in the King's left ear. And he spotted her now as she emerged.

Signor Pellegrini ran to the front of the stage. He steadied himself to catch the ballerina when she leaped back. Everyone would think this was a new act that Florabel and he had practiced in private as a surprise.

What happened next is flea history.

People were getting restless. "Where is Florabel?" they demanded, and they began stomping their feet and shouting, "Florabel! Florabel! We want Florabel!"

Florabel, seated on the King's earlobe, was enjoying all this. She delayed her return leap until she felt the most dramatic moment for it had arrived. She noted that the faithful Pellegrini was still in the limelight, still in the proper

stance, ready to receive her. And she listened with a great deal of tenderness to the speech Professor Fabadessa was now making.

Raising his hand for silence, with tears in his eyes, he made his sad announcement. "Florabel," he said. "Florabel the fabulous, the inimitable, the one and only Florabel has gone. She has out-leaped herself as we all warned her she would do someday, and she's gone!" As he spoke, the twelve-stringed orchestra made up of gifted musician fleas from Finland played a sad and mournful tune.

THAT FLORABEL!
ISNT SHE SOMETHING?
WHAT A FAR-OUT FLEA!

By now Florabel had dined luxuriously on the King's left ear, and as the King had had wine and caviar earlier in the day and Florabel had never tasted such rich fare before, she had more than enough strength for the long leap back. This moment of sad music was the right and most dramatic one in which to reappear.

As Florabel readied herself for the long leap back, poised on the tip of the King's long nose which was a better jumping-off place than his ear, a little dog underfoot suddenly let out a sharp yap, having taken an unreasonable dislike to Dandy, the King's horse. Dandy, whinnying wildly, could not be calmed. He rose up on his hind legs and then took off. The Prince's pony, Paint, panicked too, and both steeds galloped out of the Tivoli Gardens with the King and the Prince hanging on for dear life.

At first Florabel was terrified. She slipped off the King's nose, but fortunately landed in his beard where she took refuge. She resolved not to take one other bite. Gradually, the horses began to calm down, but they were still galloping along the cobblestone streets.

Getting used to the pace, Florabel began to enjoy the outing and waited excitedly for what might happen next. They were galloping past the Round Tower of Copenhagen and speeding past the little mermaid in the harbor. Feeling more daring, Florabel crept from one part of the King's head to another, not wanting to miss one single sight.

All of a sudden, she saw someone racing up from behind like a whirlwind.

"Why, it's Noble!" Florabel exclaimed.

More excitement. For Noble was a Great Dane, not an ordinary dog. He was a retired boar hunter, formerly in the employ of the King. Now he worked for Professor Fabadessa as a flea recruiter. Often he could be seen lounging in the sunshine at the waterfront, his bloodshot eyes focused on incoming ships, always on the alert for something novel in the way of traveling flea performers for his master's flea circus. "The flea catcher of Copenhagen" was Noble's nickname.

Florabel watched the speeding Great Dane, spattering up the dust, coming closer and closer. Little did she know who was astride him. But soon she found out.

Signor Pellegrini had witnessed in dismay the abduction of Florabel, accidental though it may have been, by the King of Denmark. Immediately he had leaped onto Noble's forehead, given him an urgent nip, and commanded, "Follow them!" With Pellegrini giving him bite after bite, Noble became a tornado and tore in pursuit of the royal steeds.

"Pellegrini to the rescue!" shouted the valiant flea weight lifter, as he nipped Noble sharply to make him go faster.

The Great Dane, who knew the two royal horses from boar hunts in the old days, got the message over to them that they had to turn around and go back to the Tivoli Gardens. Whinnying wildly again, the horses swerved sharply around

WHAT DOES ABDUCTION MEAN?

IT'S THE SAME AS KIDNAPPING.

and tore back to the flea circus where people still lingered. Everyone cleared the way for the onrushing horses who came to a halt directly in front of the flea circus stage, where Noble, his long tongue lolling out of the side of his mouth, had come to an abrupt stop as ordered by Signor Pellegrini.

Pellegrini was not much of a leaper. But the speed of his ride had impelled him right onto center stage where, again, he steadied himself to receive the fluttering ballerina, Florabel, as, a split second later, she leaped!

What a roar arose from the crowd then! What a tumult of praise and joy! "There she is! There she is! I see her! There's Florabel! There's Florabellissima!" These exclamations and more were recorded in the evening paper, which had to change its headline from FLORABEL LOST to FLORABEL FOUND.

Then came the grand finale—the parade around the stage, the Grand Mogul floating on a magic carpet, the ladies of the chorus dancing the minuet, the Yankee Clipper drawn across stage by Signor Pellegrini, Florabel swinging on her golden trapeze, blowing kisses and then leaping down to take bow after bow after bow.

The applause was deafening.

Naturally, after that day, Florabel became known as Princess Florabel, a name suitable for a flea who, having bitten a king, now had royal blood in her veins. She became more beloved than ever, and the rest of the troupe always saved the best bits of chocolate for her and gave her the most valentines.

Meet Your Author

Eleanor Estes

I like to do nothing. It is one of my favorite hobbies. But I don't have much time for it. When I'm doing nothing, suddenly something hops into my head that will turn into a story, the part that comes after "Once upon a time."

Take the case of *Florabel and the Fabulous Flea Circus*. I was lying on the divan on a hot day in August, and I was working on my hobby, doing nothing. Suddenly a flea leaped on my ankle and bit it.

"Oh, no!" I said out loud to myself. "The cats have fleas. Oh, my gosh!"

I didn't bother to change my dress or even to take off my apron. I ran out the door and over to Hall-Benedict Drug Store, and I bought two flea collars for my two cats, Golden Boy and Jennie; came back, and put the collars around their necks. Then I lay down again and tried to do nothing again.

But the flea bite itched, and I had to begin to think about fleas. First, I remembered that once my mother told me that dog fleas jump off dogs onto the floor or anywhere, but that cat fleas stay on cats; they don't jump off. My, was she wrong! I had a terrible flea bite, and the flea had to have leaped off Jennie or Golden Boy because we don't have a dog anymore. I wondered if the flea that bit me, a writer, might

233

turn into a writer flea. Maybe writing is catching. Maybe that same flea is writing her memoirs right now.

Then I remembered going to the flea circus in the Tivoli Gardens in Copenhagen, Denmark. And I remembered a famous singer singing *The Song of the Flea* once, and I remembered the ha-ha-ha's in that song. So now, with all these flea thoughts leaping around inside my mind, I had to stop doing nothing. I had to go to the typewriter and begin "Once there was a flea named Florabel. . . ."

And that's the story you are reading today.

Eleanor Estes has written many books you'd like to read. Look for them in your library.
The Alley
Ginger Pye
The Hundred Dresses
The Moffats
The Middle Moffat
The Witch Family
The Tunnel of Hugsy Goode
The Coat-Hanger Christmas Tree

The Snowflake

by Walter de la Mare

Before I melt,
Come, look at me!
This lovely icy filigree!
Of a great forest
In one night
I make a wilderness
Of white:
By skyey cold
Of crystals made,
All softly, on
Your finger laid,
I pause, that you
My beauty see:
Breathe, and I vanish
Instantly.

THE FLOATING GARDEN

Ryerson Johnson

You know that a board floats. Soap bubbles float. And, of course, a boat floats. What else floats? Do you think a garden could? A whole big garden with heavy dirt, and things growing in it—vegetables and flowers? Do you think a garden could float on water?

A very long time ago an Aztec Indian boy named Running Deer lived in a sunny land that is now Mexico. He lived with his father and mother and his brother and sister on the edge of a big lake. *He* didn't think a garden could float.

Of course, there was no reason why it should. Not then. His family and all the other families in their little village had

236

Illustrated by Lee Hill

good gardens that grew on the land. When Running Deer wasn't helping to tend the garden, he was out hunting rabbits in the hills.

One day he came running home to his little village by the lake. He had been running so far and so fast that he dropped to the ground. He couldn't talk at first. All he could do was try to catch his breath.

His father bent over him and took him in his arms. "What is it, son? What is the matter?"

"The warriors," he said, as soon as he could talk. "The warriors we have been hearing about. They are coming from the north. I saw them. They have spears and swords and bows and arrows—and they are killing everybody who tries to stop them!"

Running Deer stood up, still breathing hard. "Hurry!" he said. "Tell everybody. We have to run away."

His father shook his head. "We could never escape them," he said. "There are too many, and they swarm everywhere over the land. No, there is only one chance.

Quickly, warn our neighbors, and then help me carry everything we can to the boat."

Running Deer did as he was told. Then, as fast as they could, he and his family loaded their boat. At the last minute they had to throw some things away—some of their yellow squashes and corn, some of their bright and heavy woven cloth—to make room for everybody. Running Deer helped his little brother and sister into the boat, and his father and mother paddled away just as the first of the fierce warriors came over the nearest hill.

The warriors threw spears and shot arrows, but all of the boats were far out in the lake by this time. No one was hurt. No boats were sunk.

Running Deer and his family landed on a tiny island in the middle of the lake. Their friends from the village floated to other small islands near them. There they were safe.

One thing they had made sure to bring with them—seeds. The summers here were long, the sun was hot, and there was enough warm rain to make corn and beans and squash and tomatoes grow.

But there was one worrisome problem. The islands were very small. There was not enough room to grow all the food that people needed to eat. They caught some fish, but not enough. Running Deer and his brother and sister were almost always a little hungry. Running Deer knew that his mother and father were, too, because they got thinner and thinner.

"If we stay here," Running Deer's little sister said, "we'll starve."

"Yes, but we can't leave the islands," Running Deer said. "The warriors from the north are everywhere out there. They would kill us."

"What can we do?"

"I don't know," their father said, and he shook his head sadly.

But one day he had a very thoughtful look on his face. "Help me pick some water grass from the lake," he told his children.

"We can't eat water grass," Running Deer said.

"No," his father said, "but I think I have a good idea. Everybody, start picking."

At first it was fun to pick the long thick grass, or reeds, that grew out of the mud along the shallow edge of the lake. The whole family splashed around in the warm water, picking. At noon when Running Deer's mother stopped to fix some corn cakes from meal she had pounded, Running Deer said, "I'm getting tired. Don't we have enough water grass now?"

"No, no," his father said. "Not nearly enough. We have to pick until the bundles are higher than our heads."

"But that will take all day."

"It will take *many* days."

"But why do we need so much?"

"I'll show you when the time comes," said Running Deer's father. "Keep picking."

They worked many days before Running Deer's father said they had enough water grass. It took so long because they were weak and needed to rest often, for they hadn't had enough to eat. When they first came to the island, they each had four of the thin corn cakes that Running Deer's mother baked over the coals of the fire. Four at every meal, with chopped vegetables inside, green leaves and red tomatoes.

Now they each had only one corn cake, and sometimes it wasn't even folded over anything inside.

But Running Deer's father and mother remained cheerful. A soft excitement even glowed in their dark eyes as they started weaving the water grass into a shallow basket, long and wide. Running Deer and his brother and sister danced around, looking and wondering.

After covering the bottom of the basket with leaves, Running Deer's father floated it on the lake.

"If it's a new kind of boat," Running Deer said, "I don't think it will float. Water will come in between the leaves."

"It's not a boat," his father said, "and water is *supposed* to come in between the leaves and the woven grass. But the leaves will keep the mud from falling out."

"What mud?" Running Deer wanted to know.

"The mud that you and your brother and sister will bring up from the bottom of the lake and put in the basket."

That part was the most fun of all. The children splashed around in the water like turtles, bringing up mud and putting it in the big floating basket.

Running Deer's father wove a rope with some of the water grass, and tied the basket of mud to the shore. Then everybody worked to make other baskets and fill them with

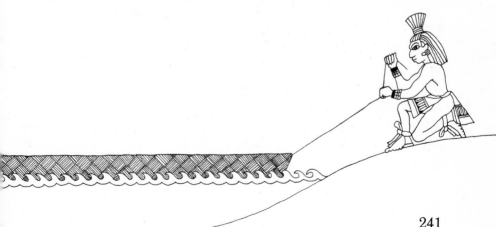

leaves and mud. These floating baskets were tied to the first one.

When the sun and wind had dried the mud enough, Running Deer's father and mother planted corn and beans and squash and tomatoes—and bright flowers—in the big floating baskets.

"It's going to be a garden!" Running Deer exclaimed. "A floating garden!"

Their Aztec neighbors on the other little islands saw what was happening, and they made garden baskets, too. The small islands grew bigger and bigger as the floating gardens reached out from their shores.

Under the hot sun the red tomatoes and the yellow squashes and all the other vegetables—and the bright flowers—grew in the floating baskets. The roots of the growing things reached down between the woven water grass, down and down through the water, all the way to the mud at the bottom of the lake. The roots grew bigger and went deeper into the mud until they were strong enough to anchor the floating gardens firmly to the shore.

Roots and leaves and sand and mud made the floating gardens almost a part of the tiny island. Within a few years bushes and even willow trees started growing. Finally the trees were rooted so strongly in the bottom of the lake that small houses could be built among the growing things in the gardens.

Always after that, whenever the Indians needed to grow more food, they just built more of the floating gardens.

Today in Mexico you can float in flat-bottomed boats or canoes in the canals of this same lake, Lake Xochimilco, and pick flowers from the floating gardens that were started by the Aztec Indians long ago.

HOW DO YOU PRONOUNCE THE NAME OF THAT LAKE?

SO-CHÉ-MILKO!

SOUNDS LIKE A NEW KIND OF ICE-CREAM SODA! HYUK HYUK!

HIS BRAIN IS IN HIS STOMACH!

Carol Of The Brown King

Langston Hughes

Of the three Wise Men
Who came to the King,
One was a brown man,
So they sing.

Of the three Wise Men
Who followed the Star,
One was a brown king
From afar.

They brought fine gifts
Of spices and gold
In jeweled boxes
Of beauty untold.

Unto His humble
Manger they came
And bowed their heads
In Jesus' name.

Three Wise Men,
One dark like me—
Part of His
Nativity.

243

Woodcut by Ann Grifalconi

FOUR-LEGS

by Tom McGowen

all-tree had killed a fine, fat bird and was on his way back to the tribal caves when he came across the wolf cub. It was lying with the back of its body pinned among the branches of a fallen tree. There had been a storm during the night, and a howl of wind had torn the dead trunk in two and sent it crashing to the ground. The frightened cub, although unhurt, had been trapped among the branches when the tree fell.

It was a very young cub and quite small, but meat was meat, and Tall-tree lifted his spear. Then he paused. It had come to him that babies have a way of growing bigger. If he kept the cub until it grew to full size, it would provide a great deal more meat.

244

Illustrated by Bob Totten

The thought seemed a good one, so Tall-tree unwrapped a strip of leather that had been twined around his forearm and tied the cub's front legs together. It growled and snapped at him, but its teeth were too small to damage his tough skin. When the animal's front legs were secured, Tall-tree heaved aside the branches and yanked the cub free. It scrabbled furiously at him with its back legs until he pinioned them, too. Then Tall-tree strode on his way.

Coming to the place of caves, he went to the great fire to turn over the results of his hunt as was the law. Old Bent-leg sat before the fire, his good leg tucked beneath him and the withered one, crushed by a bison many snows ago, stretched out. Bent-leg kept tally on the game that younger hunters brought. Tall-tree dropped the bird on the small pile of animals near the old man's leg. Bent-leg nodded, then jerked his head toward the wolf cub that hung, whining, from Tall-tree's hand.

"What is that?" grunted the old hunter.

"A small four-legs night-howler," replied Tall-tree, giving his people's name for the animal. "It came to me that I could keep it tied in my cave and feed it scraps from my own food. When it is full grown, we can kill it for its meat."

Bent-leg frowned, but then realized the cleverness of Tall-tree's thinking.

"That is good!" he exclaimed. "It is little meat now, but it will be much meat later!"

Food was always a problem for the tribe. Daily, the men hunted for animals and birds while the women and children searched for roots, berries, and insects that could be eaten. Everything that was found was shared by the tribe, and often there was hardly enough.

Tall-tree walked to his cave. Near the entrance was a large boulder, beside which he dropped the squirming cub. From the cave he brought several thin strips of animal hide. These he knotted together to make a rope, which he quickly tied around the cub's neck, avoiding its snapping teeth. Then, with a grunt, he tipped the boulder up and kicked the free end of the rope beneath it. Letting the boulder settle back with a thump, he untied the animal's legs.

The cub rolled to its feet, shook itself, and made a dash for freedom, only to have its legs jerked out from under it as the rope pulled it to an abrupt stop. Seeing that the four-legs was firmly tethered, Tall-tree nodded and reentered his cave.

The midafternoon sun was high and hot when he came
out later. Tall-tree glanced at the four-legs. Its head was
down, its tail drooped, and it panted noisily. The thought
came to Tall-tree that if he were the four-legs, tied in the hot
sun all this time, he would be thirsty. Unslinging the animal
skin water bag that hung over his shoulder, he untied its
mouth and poured a small puddle onto the ground. The cub
growled faintly, but inched forward and began to lap the
water.

Tall-tree frowned. He would often be gone for long trips,
and he wondered how to keep the cub supplied with water
during his absence. He didn't want it to die of thirst.

He went into the cave for his sharp-edged digging stone.
Outside again, he began chopping at the sandy soil. Growling, the four-legs backed away as far as the leather rope
would let it, and glared at him.

In a short time, Tall-tree had made a hole that seemed
suitably deep. He lined the hole with an animal skin,
weighting down the edges with small rocks. Then he emptied
his water bag into the hole. The skin held the water. The
four-legs now had its own water hole, which would keep it
from getting thirsty. Tall-tree grunted in approval and left.

When he returned later, he carried several meaty bones,
left from his share of food at the tribal fire. He dropped these
before the four-legs, and although it growled at him, he could
hear its teeth scraping on the bones from within his cave.

Every day thereafter Tall-tree put fresh water into the four-legs' hole, brought it scraps of meat, and cleaned up after it. After many days had passed, he noticed a change. The four-legs no longer growled at him when he came near. In fact, when it saw him coming now, it would stand and watch him, moving its tail back and forth in an odd way. Tall-tree realized it no longer feared him. He found it pleasant to have the little animal acting friendly toward him. He was surprised to find himself talking to it as though it were a child.

"Here is your meat, Four-legs," he would call as he approached with a handful of scraps. "Are you thirsty, Four-legs?" he would ask as he filled its water hole. The animal's ears would twitch and its tail would move back and forth at the sound of his voice.

And Tall-tree no longer had to guard against the cub's teeth. Instead of tossing the meat and bones to the animal, he now let the cub take them from his hand. And once, as he was filling the water hole, the four-legs pushed its nose against his hand and licked it. Tall-tree jerked his hand back in surprise. But then, hesitantly, he held it out again. Once more the pink tongue flashed out and the bushy tail fanned the air, furiously. Tall-tree grinned.

After that, he began to play a game with the wolf cub. Whenever he approached the cave, he would try to surprise the animal by coming from a different direction or by moving stealthily. But always, the four-legs would be staring straight at him, straining at the rope and beating the air with its tail.

Then, one day, Tall-tree was bringing the catch from his hunting to the fire when Bent-leg peered up at him.

"Is the four-legs fat enough?" asked Bent-leg.

Tall-tree hesitated. He had nearly forgotten his reason for keeping the cub.

"Not yet," he said, uncomfortably.

"Soon, eh?" queried Bent-leg. Tall-tree nodded and hurried away.

At his cave he squatted and looked anxiously at the wolf cub. It *had* grown, and before long it would be as big as it was going to get. Then he would have to turn it over to be meat for the tribe, as he had promised.

But he didn't want the four-legs to die. Something had happened to him and to it. Perhaps, because it had been so little when he found it, it had not grown up to be like other wolves that showed their teeth at men and ran from them. Instead of being a wild wolf, Four-legs was more like a child that liked him. And he liked it!

The next day, Tall-tree went hunting determined to bring back more game than ever before. Perhaps, he thought, if he brought plenty of meat, Bent-leg would forget about the wolf. But the hunt went badly. He returned with only a young squirrel. And to his dismay, none of the other hunters had fared well, either. The pile of birds and animals by the fire was smaller than usual.

"It is not enough!" said Bent-leg. "We must have the four-legs now, Tall-tree."

"Wait a few days," said Tall-tree. "The hunting may grow even harder. We may need the four-legs even more then."

Bent-leg did not press him, so he hurried away. At his cave he knelt beside the wolf and rubbed its head. It nudged him with a cold nose and swept the ground with its tail.

That night, lying beside the fire in his cave, he knew that the next day, or the day after that, he would have to give the wolf to the tribe. Dreading the dawn, he fell asleep.

It seemed only seconds later that something suddenly awakened him. It was Four-legs, snarling furiously.

Tall-tree was on his feet in an instant. Snatching his spear, he peered over the nearly dead fire. In the moonlight Four-legs stood before the cave, snarling and showing its teeth, its fur bristling. Beyond it, green eyes gleamed and scales glinted on a long, sinuous body. There was an evil hiss and a rattling sound. The hair at the back of Tall-tree's neck rose as he saw the great snake, poised to sink its poisonous fangs into the wolf's body.

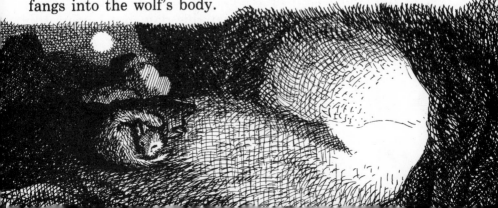

Tall-tree exploded into action. Leaping over the fire, he swung his spear forward like a club, slamming it into the snake's body, just below the swaying head. The heavy blow knocked the serpent writhing to the ground. Springing after it, Tall-tree smashed the spear again and again into the snake's head.

After a time, Tall-tree leaned on his spear, panting heavily. Although the snake's body still feebly twisted, he knew it was dead. Four-legs knew it was dead, too, and stopped growling.

Tall-tree knew what had happened. Drawn by the heat of the fire, the snake had crawled toward the cave. It would have been attracted by the warmth of Tall-tree's body and probably would have coiled itself next to him. Had he jostled it, the creature would have bitten him. He remembered when just such a snake had bitten a man, who had raved with pain and then died. Tall-tree shivered. If Four-legs had not growled and wakened him, he also might have died.

Tall-tree fed the fire until it blazed up again. Then he dragged the snake into the cave and began to skin it. When he finished, he gazed thoughtfully at the thick coils of white meat.

At dawn, he hurried to the tribal fire, carrying the snake meat. Bent-leg was already there, as were several hunters, waiting for a lighter sky before starting on their way. Among them was Green-leaf, the tribe's leader. Tall-tree dumped the coils of meat near Bent-leg's feet.

"I have meat for the tribe," he said, looking at Green-leaf. "I will hunt for other meat this day, but I bring this meat now."

The men stared at the white coils. "Where did you find this long-crawler?" asked Green-leaf.

"It came to my cave, seeking warmth as long-crawlers do after sundown," Tall-tree replied. "I killed it."

"Were you bitten?" asked Green-leaf, looking at him anxiously.

Tall-tree shook his head. "I might have been bitten," he said. "But the four-legs tied at my cave woke me with the noise of its anger. It saved my life." He looked into Green-leaf's eyes. "I was going to give the four-legs as meat for the tribe. Let me give this meat instead, Green-leaf. Let the four-legs live!"

Green-leaf considered his words. "I do not know what an animal is good for, except to eat. What will you do with the four-legs?"

"I will set it free," answered Tall-tree.

The chieftain thought. "It is well," he said at last. "You promised the tribe meat, and you brought more meat than you promised. The four-legs saved you to hunt for the tribe. Let it go then, if that is your wish."

Tall-tree walked slowly back to his cave. He was glad that the wolf would not have to die. Yet he felt as though a big stone sat heavily inside his chest. He knew that when he untied Four-legs' rope, the wolf would run off into the forest. Tall-tree did not like this thought, but he felt he must set Four-legs free. It was the only way he could repay the animal for saving his life.

At the cave, he knelt, loosened the knot in the leather rope, and pulled it off Four-legs' neck. The wolf shook itself and looked at him. Tall-tree turned and went into the cave. He felt a wetness in his eyes, something he had not felt since he was a boy. He squatted by the fire and gathered his weapons for the day's hunt.

Something pattered over the cave floor behind him.

Tall-tree turned. Four-legs stood just inside the cave opening. Its tail drooped and it held its head low. Its brown eyes stared into Tall-tree's black ones.

Then the animal moved into the cave. It was a strange movement. Its stomach was on the ground, but the back part of its body was pointed upward. It inched forward with little pulls of its front paws. Slowly, it crept toward Tall-tree until its nose was only inches from the man's face.

Then it licked Tall-tree's nose.

Tall-tree yelled with delight. Four-legs didn't want to leave; it had said so as plainly as if it could talk! Tall-tree rubbed the animal's head with both hands. Four-legs flopped onto its back, and Tall-tree rubbed its stomach. The wolf's tongue lolled out of its mouth, and its lips were pulled back into what seemed to be a grin as wide as the one on Tall-tree's face.

After a while Tall-tree jumped to his feet. "Come on, Four-legs," he said. "Let's go hunting!"

Four-legs rolled to its feet and shook itself. Then the world's first pet and its two-legged friend happily hurried off together.

Old Cricket says

Suppose you were an English child living 500 years ago. In that long-ago time there were no storybooks or magazines like Cricket for you to read. But many writers—mostly poets—wrote Books of Courtesy, as they were called, which taught manners to those girls and boys who were later to become important ladies and gentlemen.

Here are some of the things you would have to remember, if you were learning your table manners in a great English house.

First, don't sit down before the master of the house has done so. Don't lean your elbow on the table. Never spit on the table or pick your nose or ears or scratch yourself. Also, you must not put your fingers in your dish or eat your meat too quickly or drink anything while your mouth is full of food. Your hands must be clean, especially your fingernails. You have no fork. But you do have a knife, and you must not pick your teeth with it. Don't cool your meat or your drink by blowing on it. And don't throw bones on the floor, please, or pet the dog who's probably waiting for them. Or lick dishes, for only cats do that.

Does it sound as though table manners have changed much in 500 years?

Old Cricket

Tea Party

Mister Beedle Baddlebug,
Don't bundle up in your boodlebag
Or numble in your jimblejug;
Now eat your nummy tiffletag
Or I will never invite you
To tea again with me. Shoo!

Harry Behn

Owls In the Family
Farley Mowat

When Farley Mowat was a boy, he lived in Saskatoon, a prairie town in Saskatchewan, Canada. In this story he tells about his pet horned owls named Wol and Weeps.

Wol and Weeps were with us long enough to be well known in Saskatoon. Particularly Wol. As my father said, Wol never quite realized he was an owl. Most of the time he seemed to think he was people. At any rate, he liked being with people and he wanted to be with us so much that we finally had to stop trying to keep him out of the house. If we locked him out, he would come and bang his big beak against the windowpanes so hard we were afraid the glass would break. Screens were no good either, because he would tear them open with one sweep of his big claws. So eventually he became a house owl.

258

WHO DREW THESE PICTURES, LADYBUG?

James Arnosky
WHO IS BOTH
TALENTED AN
PERSISTE

He was always very well mannered in the house and caused no trouble—except on one particular occasion.

One midsummer day we had a visit from the new minister of our church. He had just arrived in Saskatoon, so he didn't know about our owls. Mother took him into the living room, and he sat down on our sofa with a cup of tea balanced on his knee, and began to talk to Mother about me skipping Sunday School.

Wol had been off on an expedition down on the river bank. When he got home, he ambled across the lawn, jumped up to the ledge of one of the living room windows, and peered in. Spotting the stranger, he gave another leap and landed heavily on the minister's shoulder.

Mother had seen him coming and had tried to warn the minister, but she was too late. By the time she had her mouth open, Wol was already hunched down on the man's shoulder, peering around into his face, making friendly owl noises.

"*Who-who?*" he asked politely.

Instead of answering, the minister let out a startled yelp and sprang to his feet. The tea spilled all over the rug, and the teacup shot into the fireplace and smashed into a million pieces.

It was all so sudden that Wol lost his balance; and when he lost his balance, his talons just naturally tightened up to help him steady himself. When Wol tightened his grip, the minister gave a wild yell and made a dash for the door.

Wol had never been treated this way before. He didn't like it. Just as the minister reached the front porch, Wol spread his wings and took off. His wings were big, and they were strong too. One of them clipped the man a bang on the side of his head, making him yell even louder. But by then

Wol was airborne. He flew up into his favorite poplar tree, and he was in such a huff at the way he had been treated that he wouldn't come down again till after supper.

Riding on people's shoulders was a favorite pastime with Wol. Usually he was so careful with his big claws that you couldn't even feel them. Sometimes when he was on your shoulder and feeling specially friendly, he would nibble your ear. His beak was sharp enough to have taken the ear right off your head at a single bite, but he would just catch the bottom of your ear in his beak and very gently nibble it a little. It didn't hurt at all, though it used to make some people nervous. One of my father's friends was a man who worked for the railroad, and he had very big, red ears. Every time he came for a visit to our house he wore a cap—a cap with earflaps. He wore it even in summertime because, he said, with ears as big as his and an ear-nibbling owl around he just couldn't afford to take chances.

Wol was usually good-natured, but he *could* get mad. One morning Mother sent me to the store for some groceries. My bike had a flat tire so I had to walk, and Wol walked with me. We were only a little way from our house when we met the postman coming toward us. He had a big bundle of letters in his hand, and he was sorting them and not watching where he was going. Instead of stepping around Wol, he walked right into him.

Worse still, he didn't even look down to see what it was he had stumbled over. He just gave a kind of kick to get whatever it was out of his way.

Well, you could do a lot of things to Wol and get away with it—but kicking him was something different. Hissing

like a giant teakettle, he spread his wings wide out and clomped the postman on the shins with them. A whack from one of his wings was like the kick of a mule. The postman dropped his handful of letters and went pelting down the street, yelling blue murder—with Wol right on his heels.

After I got hold of Wol and calmed him down, I apologized to the postman. But for a month after that he wouldn't come into our yard at all. He used to stand at the gate and whistle until one of us came out to get the mail.

Our owls were so used to going nearly everywhere with me now that when school started that fall I had a hard time keeping them at home. I used to bicycle to school, which was about two miles away across the river. During the first week after school opened, I was late four times because of having to take the owls back home after they had followed me part way.

Finally Dad suggested that I lock them up in the big pen each morning just before I left. Wol and Weeps hadn't used that pen for a long time; and when I put them in, they acted as if it were a jail. Wol was particularly furious, and he began to tear at the chicken wire with his beak and claws. I sneaked off fast. I was almost late anyway, and I knew if I was late once more I'd be kept in after school.

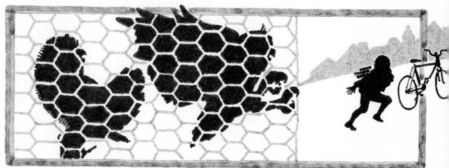

I was about halfway over the river bridge when a man on the footpath gave a shout and pointed to something behind my back. At the same moment a car, coming toward me, jammed on its brakes and nearly skidded into the cement railings. Not knowing what was going on, I put on my brakes too, and I just had time to stop when there was a wild rush of air on the back of my neck, a deep "Hooo-Hooo-Hooo!" in my ear, and Wol landed on my shoulder.

He was out of breath—but he was so pleased with himself that I didn't have the heart to take him home. Anyway, there wasn't time. So he rode the handlebars the rest of the way to school.

I skidded into the yard just as the two-minute bell was ringing and all the other kids were going through the doors. I couldn't decide what on earth to do with Wol. Then I remembered that I had some twine in my pocket. I fished it out and used it to tie him by one leg to the handlebars.

The first class I had that morning was French. Well, between worrying about Wol and not having done my homework, I was soon in trouble with the teacher (whom we called Fifi behind her back). Fifi made me come up in front of the class so she could tell me how dumb I was. I was standing beside her desk, wishing the floor would open and swallow me up, when there was a whump-whump-whump at the window. I turned my head to look, and there sat Wol.

It hadn't taken him long to untie the twine.

I heard later that he had banged on the windows of two or three other classrooms before he found the right one. Having found the right room at last, he didn't waste any time. Unluckily Fifi had left one of our windows open. Wol ducked down, saw me, and flew right in.

He was probably aiming to land on my shoulder, but he missed and at the last second tried to land on Fifi's desk. It was a polished hardwood desk; he couldn't get a grip on it. His brakes just wouldn't hold; he skated straight across the desk, scattering papers and books all over the floor. Fifi saw him coming and tried to get up out of her chair, but she wasn't fast enough. Wol skidded off the end of the desk and plumped right into her lap.

There were some ructions after that. I was sent to the principal's office, and Fifi went home for the rest of the day.

The principal was a good fellow, though. He just read me a lecture, and warned me that if I didn't keep my owl away from the school in future, he would have to get the police to do something about it.

We finally figured out a way to keep the owls from following me to school. Each morning, just before I left, we would let Wol and Weeps into the kitchen. Mother would feed them the bacon rinds left over from breakfast, while I sneaked out the front door and rode away. It worked fine, but it was a little hard on Mother because the owls got so fond of the kitchen she usually couldn't get them out of it again. Once I heard her telling a friend that, until a woman had tried to bake a cake with two horned owls looking over her shoulders, she hadn't really lived at all!

Why the Sky Is Blue

John Ciardi

I don't suppose you happen to know
Why the sky is blue? It's because the snow
Takes out the white. That leaves it clean
For the trees and grass to take out the green.
Then pears and bananas start to mellow
And bit by bit they take out the yellow.
The sunsets, of course, take out the red
And pour it into the ocean bed
Or behind the mountains in the west.
You take all that out and the rest
Couldn't be anything else but blue.

—Look for yourself. You can see it's true.

CRICKET and LADYBUG

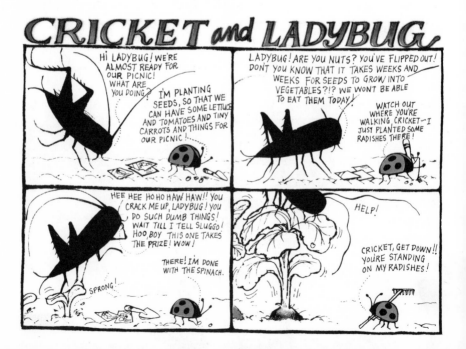

meet my folks!
by Ted Hughes

I've heard so much about other folks' folks—
How somebody's Uncle told such jokes
The cat split laughing and had to be stitched,
How somebody's Aunt got so bewitched
She fried the kettle and washed the water
And spanked a letter and posted her daughter.
Other folks' folks get so well known,
And nobody knows about my own.

267

WOW!
HE'S AN
M.S.I.A.!

George Adamson
DREW
THESE PICTURES!

THAT MEANS A
MOST SURPRISING, INTERESTING ARTIST!

My Sister Jane

And I say nothing—no, not a word
About our Jane. Haven't you heard?
She's a bird, a bird, a bird, a bird.
Oh it never would do to let folks know
My sister's nothing but a great big crow.

Each day (we daren't send her to school)
She pulls on stockings of thick blue wool
To make her pin crow legs look right,
Then fits a wig of curls on tight,
And dark spectacles—a huge pair
To cover her very crowy stare.
Oh it never would do to let folks know
My sister's nothing but a great big crow.

When visitors come she sits upright
(With her wings and her tail tucked out of sight).
They think her queer but extremely polite.
Then when the visitors have gone
She whips out her wings and with her wig on
Whirls through the house at the height of your head—
Duck, duck, or she'll knock you dead.
Oh it never would do to let folks know
My sister's nothing but a great big crow.

At meals whatever she sees she'll stab it—
Because she's a crow and that's a crow habit.
My mother says, "Jane! Your manners! Please!"
Then she'll sit quietly on the cheese,
Or play the piano nicely by dancing on the keys—
Oh it never would do to let folks know
My sister's nothing but a great big crow.

My Uncle Dan

My Uncle Dan's an inventor, you may think that's very fine.
You may wish he was your uncle instead of being mine—
If he wanted he could make a watch that bounces when it
drops,
He could make a helicopter out of string and bottle tops
Or any really useful thing you can't get in the shops.
       But Uncle Dan has other ideas:
       The bottomless glass for ginger beers,
       The toothless saw that's safe for the tree,
       A special word for a spelling bee
       (Like Lionocerangoutangadder),
       Or the roll-uppable rubber ladder,
       The mystery pie that bites when it's bit—
       My Uncle Dan invented it.
My Uncle Dan sits in his den inventing night and day.
His eyes peer from his hair and beard like mice from a load of
hay.
And does he make the shoes that will go on walks without
your feet?
A shrinker to shrink instantly the elephants you meet?
A carver that just carves from the air steaks cooked and
ready to eat?
       No, no, he has other intentions—
       Only perfectly useless inventions:
       Glassless windows (they never break),
       A medicine to cure the earthquake,
       The unspillable screwed-down cup,
       The stairs that go neither down nor up,
       The door you simply paint on a wall—
       Uncle Dan invented them all.

My Father

Some fathers work at the office, others work at the store,
Some operate great cranes and build up skyscrapers galore,
Some work in canning factories counting green peas into cans,
Some drive all night in huge and thundering removal vans.

> But mine has the strangest job of the lot.
> My father's the Chief Inspector of—What?
> O don't tell the mice, don't tell the moles,
> My father's the Chief Inspector of HOLES.

It's a work of the highest importance because you never know
What's in a hole, what fearful thing is creeping from below.

HULLO? YOO HOO!
ARE YOU THERE, GEORGE?
THE INSPECTOR IS COMING
TO LOOK AT YOUR HOLE!

OH, YEAH? WELL, HE'D
BETTER NOT MESS UP
MY LIVING-ROOM! I JUST CLEANED IT!

Perhaps it's a hole to the ocean and will soon gush water in tons,
Or maybe it leads to a vast cave full of gold and skeletons.

Though a hole might seem to have nothing but dirt in,
Somebody's simply got to make certain.
Caves in the mountain, clefts in the wall,
My father has to inspect them all.

That crack in the road looks harmless. My father knows it's not.
The world may be breaking into two and starting at that spot.
Or maybe the world is a great egg, and we live on the shell,
And it's just beginning to split and hatch: you simply cannot tell.

If you see a crack, run to the phone, run!
My father will know just what's to be done.
A rumbling hole, a silent hole,
My father will soon have it under control.

Keeping a check on all these holes he hurries from morning to night.
There might be sounds of marching in one, or an eye shining bright.
A tentacle came groping from a hole that belonged to a mouse,
A floor collapsed and Chinamen swarmed up into the house.

A hole's an unpredictable thing—
Nobody knows what a hole might bring.
Caves in the mountain, clefts in the wall,
My father has to inspect them all!

273

YOU'RE ENGLISH, MUFFIN — SO WHAT'S A "REMOVAL VAN"?

IN AMERICA, YOU'D SAY "MOVING VAN" OR "MOVING TRUCK" IN ENGLAND, WE CALL TRUCKS "VANS" OR "LORRIES".

I WANT YOU TO MEET...
BY DAVID McCORD

. . . Meet Ladybug,
her little sister Sadiebug,
her mother, Mrs. Gradybug,
her aunt, that nice oldmaidybug,
and Baby—she's a fraidybug.

"W"

by James Reeves

The King sent for his wise men all
  To find a rhyme for W;
When they had thought a good long time
But could not think of a single rhyme,
  "I'm sorry," said he, "to trouble you."

BEFORE I COUNT FIFTEEN

By Michael Rosen

If you don't put your shoes
on before I count fifteen then
we won't go to the woods
to climb the chestnut—
One

But I can't find them

Two

I can't

They're under the sofa—
Three

No

Oh yes—
Four, five, six

Stop—they've got knots,
They've got knots

You should untie the laces
when you take your shoes off—
Seven

Will you do one shoe while
I do the other then?

Eight—
But that would be cheating

Please

All right

It always . . .

275

These tiny drawings are by tiny Karen Gundersheimer

Nine

It always sticks—
I'll use my teeth

Ten

It won't, it won't
It has—look

Eleven

I'm not wearing any socks

Twelve

Stop counting, stop counting.
Mom, where are my socks,
Mom?

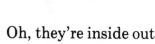

They're in your shoes
Where you left them

I didn't

Thirteen

Oh, they're inside out
and upside down
and bundled up

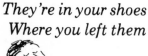

Fourteen

Have you done the knot
on the shoe you were . . .

Yes
Put it on the right foot

But socks don't have a
right and wrong foot

The shoe, silly—
Fourteen and a half

I am, I am. Wait.
Don't go to the woods
without me. Look,
that's one shoe already

Fourteen and three-quarters

There

You haven't tied
the bows yet

We could do them
on the way there

No we won't—
Fourteen and seven-eighths

Help me then
You know I'm not fast at bows

Fourteen and
Fifteen-sixteeeenths

A single bow is
all right, isn't it?

Fifteen—we're off

See, I did it.
Didn't I?

The Missing Slice

Martin Gardner

A slice is obviously missing from the cake in the above drawing. To find the piece, turn the picture upside down.

Here is the explanation of this startling optical illusion: When we turn the picture upside down, it is still possible to view it as an inverted cake with a missing slice. But since we almost never see a cake from this odd angle, we seem to see the side of a cake pan viewed from above. As a result, the straight lines are seen as a solid slice of cake rather than as an empty space, left by a slice that has been taken out.

Me and the Ecology Bit

by Joan Lexau

S ure is hard to get people to work for ecology. Everybody is in favor of it but nobody wants to do anything about it. At least I'm doing something, going around telling people what they should do. But all I get is a lot of back talk.

I have this paper route. My father had one when he was a kid so he made me get one last year. Between it and my homework, I hardly have time for playing ball and stuff. Some days I only get in a few innings.

But anyhow, on Saturdays when I collect, I put in a good word for ecology. Like last Saturday morning. It was a good collecting day. It had just turned spring and a lot of people were outside.

I went to Mr. Williams' house. As usual, he tries to pretend he's not home. But I see him burning leaves in the backyard so he's stuck. He pays me, and I tell him, "You

YEAH.

Marvin Friedman DREW THESE PICTURES! HE'S WITTY, TALENTED AND HANDSOME!

279

shouldn't burn those leaves. It's bad for the air, bad ecology. You should make a compost pile like we do. Put in the leaves, garbage, and stuff. Good for the garden."

He doesn't agree or hang his head in shame. He says, "That compost pile is your job at home, Jim, isn't it?"

"Yes," I say proudly, which would shock the heck out of my old man. He somehow has the idea I hate working with compost. Which I do.

Mr. Williams says, "Well, why don't you take a little more trouble with it, put enough dirt on top of each layer? And turn it over now and then? Then we wouldn't have this nose pollution."

"Huh?" I say. "You mean noise pollution."

"No," he says. "I mean your compost smells up the whole street."

My feelings are hurt, but that doesn't stop me from trying again. I go to collect from Ms. Greene. I have to call her Ms. Greene because if I call her Mrs., she says she doesn't have change to pay me.

She is putting her garbage out for the weekly pickup on Monday. She goes away weekends so Saturdays and Sundays we have to look at the big plastic garbage bags on her lawn. But I don't say anything about it, I just look at the garbage.

She says to me, "Go pick up that gum wrapper you threw on my lawn. Put it in one of the plastic bags. Didn't anybody teach you not to litter?"

I hold my temper and go pick up my gum wrapper and put it in a bag.

Then she says, "And there's a law in this town about keeping dogs on a leash. So why is yours always all over the place? That dog digs up my garden and messes up my yard, and last weekend Mr. Williams saw it tear open one of my garbage bags."

"Well," I say, but I can't think of anything to go with it. Then I see she is piling newspapers next to her garbage bags.

"Listen, Ms. Greene," I say, "save those papers for the school pickup and they can be made into new paper. Save aluminum cans, too."

"Like the last school pickup?" she asks. "When you said you'd come pick them up and you never showed up? It's easier to throw them away a few at a time than have a big mess like that."

I get tired trying to get Ms. Greene to do something about ecology. I go to Mr. Johnson's house. He makes a run for his car, but I can run faster than he can.

"Just trying to get to the post office before it closes," he says, huffing and puffing.

"You got time," I say. "You even got time to walk. It's only two blocks. You shouldn't take your car when you don't need to. The walk would be good exercise and save on gas. And not pollute. That's ecology."

"How about trees?" he asks me. "Are trees ecology?"

"They sure are," I say. "We had a lot about trees and ecology in school. They make the air better and stuff like that."

"See that tree over there?" he says, pointing to where there isn't any tree.

"I don't see any tree," I tell him.

"Of course not," he says. "And no grass either. Because you made a path there taking a shortcut from Mrs. Greene's. There was a little tree just starting to get bigger there until you killed it by trying to jump over it every day. Remember?"

"Oh," I say.

"And talking about not driving when you can walk. You drive your motorbike round and round your backyard all summer. And your snowmobile all winter. Isn't that wasting power and making noise pollution too?"

"But it's fun," I say.

"Well, I enjoy taking the car to the post office," he says.

"But now you've made me too late." He goes in the house looking very mad.

Then I remember he hasn't paid me. But I decide to wait until next Saturday. At least I made him not pollute with his car for once.

I don't talk to the rest of my route about ecology. It's very tiring work, this ecology bit.

But when I get home, I see my mother using the electric mixer.

"You should do that with your old egg beater," I point out to her. "Save on electricity. Women use too many electric things."

She says in a very cold voice, "So who watches TV twenty-seven hours a day around here? Or is that some other kind of electricity?"

See what I mean? Nobody's willing to do anything about ecology. Except me. And nobody listens to me.

CATS

by *Gina Ruck-Pauquèt*

Translated by Doris Orgel

What are their private and secret addresses?
Do their purrs equal our please's and yes's?
How do they produce those purrs?
At night, could they take off their furs?
And why do they sit on the roof?
Are they aloof?
Can they be sad? Do they think very much
About mouse tails and such?
Do they dance the Tom-Tango
And Feline-Fandango,
Or are they far too reserved?
What makes their claws be so curved?
How do they kindle the blaze in their eyes?
Do they wait until moonrise,
And kindle the blaze with a beam?
What do they dream?
And why don't they smile
Even once in a while?
And where do they go when they vanish for days?
Try asking a cat, and see what she says!

ERIK BLEGVAD

a true story by Ruskin Bond

The Day Grandfather Tickled a Tiger

Timothy, our tiger cub, was found by my grandfather on a hunting expedition in the Terai jungles near Dehra, in northern India. Because Grandfather lived in Dehra and knew the jungles well, he was persuaded to accompany the hunting party.

Grandfather, strolling down a forest path some distance from the main party, discovered a little abandoned tiger about eighteen inches long, hidden among the roots of a banyan tree. After the expedition ended, Grandfather took the tiger home to Dehra, where Grandmother gave him the name Timothy.

Timothy's favorite place in the house was the living room. He would snuggle down comfortably on the sofa, reclining there with serene dignity and snarling only when anyone tried to take his place. One of his chief amusements was to stalk whoever was playing with him, and so, when I

Jan Adkins DREW THESE PICTURES!

went to live with my grandparents, I became one of the tiger's pets. With a crafty look in his eyes, and his body in a deep crouch, he would creep closer and closer to me, suddenly making a dash for my feet. Then, rolling on his back and kicking with delight, he would pretend to bite my ankles.

By this time he was the size of a full-grown golden retriever, and when I took him for walks in Dehra, people on the road would give us a wide berth. At night he slept in the quarters of our cook, Mahmoud. "One of these days,"Grandmother declared, "we are going to find Timothy sitting on Mahmoud's bed and no sign of Mahmoud!"

When Timothy was about six months old, his stalking became more serious and he had to be chained up more frequently. Even the household started to mistrust him and, when he began to trail Mahmoud around the house with what looked like villainous intent, Grandfather decided it was time to transfer Timothy to a zoo.

The nearest zoo was at Lucknow, some two hundred miles away. Grandfather reserved a first-class compartment on the train for himself and Timothy and set forth. The Lucknow zoo authorities were only too pleased to receive a well-fed and fairly civilized tiger.

Grandfather had no opportunity to see how Timothy was getting on in his new home until about six months later, when he and Grandmother visited relatives in Lucknow. Grandfather went to the zoo and directly to Timothy's cage. The tiger was there, crouched in a corner, full-grown, his magnificent striped coat gleaming with health.

"Hello, Timothy," Grandfather said.

Climbing the railing, he put his arms through the bars of the cage. Timothy approached, and allowed Grandfather to put both arms about his head. Grandfather stroked the tiger's forehead and tickled his ears. Each time Timothy growled, Grandfather gave him a smack across the mouth, which had been his way of keeping the tiger quiet when he lived with us.

Timothy licked Grandfather's hands. Then he showed nervousness, springing away when a leopard in the next cage snarled at him, but Grandfather shooed the leopard off and Timothy returned to licking his hands. Every now and then the leopard would rush at the bars, and Timothy would again slink back to a neutral corner.

A number of people had gathered to watch the reunion, when a keeper pushed his way through the crowd and asked Grandfather what he was doing. "I'm talking to Timothy," said Grandfather. "Weren't you here when I gave him to the zoo six months ago?"

"I haven't been here very long," said the surprised keeper. "Please continue your conversation. I have never been able to touch that tiger myself. I find him very bad-tempered."

Grandfather had been stroking and slapping Timothy for about five minutes when he noticed another keeper observing him with some alarm. Grandfather recognized him as the keeper who had been there when he had delivered Timothy to the zoo. "You remember me," said Grandfather. "Why don't you transfer Timothy to a different cage, away from this stupid leopard?"

"But—sir," stammered the keeper. "It is not your tiger."

"I realize that he is no longer mine," said Grandfather testily. "But at least take my suggestion."

"I remember your tiger very well," said the keeper. "He died two months ago."

"Died!" exclaimed Grandfather.

"Yes, sir, of pneumonia. This tiger was trapped in the hills only last month, and he is very dangerous!"

The tiger was still licking Grandfather's arms and apparently enjoying it more all the time. Grandfather withdrew his hands from the cage in a motion that seemed to take an age. With his face near the tiger's he mumbled, "Goodnight, Timothy." Then, giving the keeper a scornful look, Grandfather walked briskly out of the zoo.

Check
James Stephens

The Night was creeping on the ground!
She crept, and did not make a sound

Until she reached the tree: And then
She covered it, and stole again

Along the grass beside the wall!
—I heard the rustling of her shawl

As she threw blackness everywhere
Along the sky, the ground, the air,

And in the room where I was hid!
But, no matter what she did

To everything that was without,
She could not put my candle out!

So I stared at the Night! And she
Stared back solemnly at me!

Illustrated by Bob Totte

Prize-Winning Contributors to Cricket's Choice

Lloyd Alexander: National Book Award; John Newbery Medal; Jewish
    Book Council Award

Hans Baumann: Mildred L. Batchelder Award; Gerstäcker-Preis

Natalie Savage Carlson: Child Study Association Award

Kornei Chukovsky: Order of Lenin

John Ciardi: Rutgers Award

Ann Nolan Clark: John Newbery Medal; Regina Medal

Elizabeth Coatsworth: John Newbery Medal

e. e. cummings: Bollingen Prize

Walter de la Mare: Carnegie Medal

T. S. Eliot: Nobel Prize

Eleanor Estes: John Newbery Medal

Robert Frost: Pulitzer Prize

Jean Craighead George: John Newbery Medal; George G. Stone
    Center Award

Joan Lexau: Child Study Association Award

Arnold Lobel: Irma Simonton Black Award; Christopher Award

Farley Mowat: Canadian Library Award

Philippa Pearce: Carnegie Medal

Alf Prøysen: Norwegian Ministry Prize

Gianni Rodari: Hans Christian Andersen Award; Premio Castello

Carl Sandburg: Pulitzer Prize

Isaac Bashevis Singer: National Book Award